Preface

The Department of Defense (DoD) purchases an enormous amount of goods and services from tens of thousands of contractors. In fiscal year (FY) 2011, DoD awarded $375.4 billion in prime contracts for weapons, other goods, and services. Most of these purchases are from a relatively small number of suppliers; just ten suppliers accounted for more than one-third of DoD purchases in FY 2011.

The possible challenges that suppliers that have not traditionally done business with DoD may have in contracting with DoD led Congress to request, in the National Defense Authorization Act (NDAA) for FY 2011, that the Secretary of Defense "review barriers to firms that are not traditional suppliers to the Department of Defense wishing to contract with the Department of Defense and its defense supply centers and develop a set of recommendations on the elimination of such barriers." DoD in turn asked the RAND Corporation to examine this issue.[1] As specified in the NDAA, we consider a firm to be a nontraditional supplier of DoD "if it does not currently have contracts and subcontracts to perform work for the Department of Defense with a total combined value in excess of $500,000."

This report should be of interest to individuals concerned with barriers to nontraditional suppliers as well as to all businesses seeking DoD contracts.

This research was sponsored by the DoD Office of Small Business Programs and conducted within the Acquisition and Technology Policy Center of the RAND National Defense Research Institute, a federally funded research and development center sponsored by the Office of the Secretary of Defense, the Joint Staff, the Unified Combatant Commands, the Department of the Navy, the Marine Corps, the defense agencies, and the defense Intelligence Community.

For more information on the RAND Acquisition and Technology and Policy Center, see http://www.rand.org/nsrd/ndri/centers/atp.html or contact the director (contact information is provided on the web page).

---

[1]   The time line for this research was extended to account for hearings by the House Armed Services Committee addressing this topic (described in the report).

RAND NATIONAL DEFENSE RESEARCH INSTITUTE

Identifying and Eliminating Barriers Faced by Nontraditional Department of Defense Suppliers

Amy G. Cox, Nancy Y. Moore, Clifford A. Grammich

Prepared for the Office of the Secretary of Defense

Approved for public release; distribution unlimited

For more information on this publication, visit www.rand.org/t/rr267

Library of Congress Cataloging-in-Publication Data

ISBN: 978-0-8330-8044-8

Published by the RAND Corporation, Santa Monica, Calif.

© Copyright 2014 RAND Corporation

RAND® is a registered trademark.

Support RAND

Make a tax-deductible charitable contribution at
www.rand.org/giving/contribute

www.rand.org

Contents

Tables

Summary

The Department of Defense (DoD) purchases an enormous amount of goods and services in more than 1,000 different industries. Although the supply base providing these goods and services is very broad, there is a large degree of concentration in it. The top ten contractors, for example, provide almost one-third of DoD goods and services, and the 40 largest account for more than half. Such concentration can make it difficult for firms outside the traditional DoD supply base to enter it, and DoD purchasing practices can compound these difficulties.

The challenges that suppliers that have not traditionally done business with DoD may have in contracting with DoD led Congress to request a review of barriers to such firms. DoD in turn asked the RAND Corporation to examine this issue as part of its review. In response, we reviewed past findings on contracting challenges for nontraditional suppliers, identified industries where DoD may most wish to develop nontraditional suppliers, and interviewed representatives of such suppliers and DoD personnel for their perceptions of barriers faced by such firms. Our definition of nontraditional suppliers comes from the legislation authorizing this research and includes entities with less than $500,000 in DoD contracts and subcontracts in the previous year.

Previous Assessments of Barriers

Attracting nontraditional suppliers has been a recurring issue for policymakers, partly because few DoD-wide policy changes have been made regarding barriers that have been already identified. This may be because making such changes is particularly difficult in a contracting environment with many goals, including inclusive and open competition, transparency, and prevention of waste, fraud, and abuse over other priorities (e.g., broadening the industrial supply base). Several reviews of nontraditional barriers have already been conducted. We summarize the barriers they identified below.

Perhaps the most prevalent concern over time has been the federal government's cumbersome and lengthy bid and selection processes, which often require that bidders have specialized units or employees. Another recurring theme is the lack of visibility, communication, or information, including a lack of access points into DoD and for design specifications. Prior reviews of barriers to nontraditional suppliers have also pointed to DoD's unique cost-accounting procedures and restricted or limited commercial opportunities for DoD products, such as international sales restrictions. Companies may also have concerns about federal funding uncertainty and about a loss of intellectual property or proprietary data. Some have claimed that there is inadequate support for developing new technology, particularly between initial research and prototype development, and some nontraditional suppliers that are small businesses have also perceived a DoD preference for larger suppliers. Finally, others have suggested that DoD personnel capabilities may need to improve to allow nontraditional suppliers to participate in requests for proposals (RFPs).

The history of barriers facing nontraditional suppliers to DoD raises several questions. First, what is the status of these barriers; do they continue to persist? Second, if they persist, are they intractable or can DoD take actions to address them and thereby expand its supply base? Third, do nontraditional suppliers face new or additional barriers to entry into the military marketplace?

Interviews with Nontraditional Suppliers and DoD Staff

To identify the status of potential barriers, we sought the concerns of nontraditional suppliers and the experience of related DoD staff. We interviewed companies in industries where DoD indicated that it wants to seek substantial innovation from nontraditional suppliers and DoD personnel in offices related to the companies interviewed. Our review of the literature and other documentation on DoD future technology needs led us to identify three such industries.

- Search, Detection, Navigation, Guidance, Aeronautical, and Nautical System and Instrument Manufacturing (North American Industry Classification System [NAICS] code 334511)
- Custom Computer Programming Services (NAICS code 541511)
- Research and Development in the Physical, Engineering, and Life Sciences (except Biotechnology) (NAICS code 541712).

We further used the Central Contractor Registration to identify firms in these industries that had less than $500,000 in contracts with DoD in the past year. We found 141 firms, and we interviewed representatives from 16. We also interviewed three DoD staff members who dealt with nontraditional suppliers for their perspective on barriers. Because these interviews are qualitative, they may or may not be representative of all nontraditional suppliers and of all DoD staff who work with nontraditional suppliers. The findings yield insight into the problem of barriers to nontraditional DoD suppliers, not statistically significant results. Nonetheless, we heard substantial repetition in the interviews, which indicates some level of shared experience.

Nontraditional Suppliers' Perceptions of Common Barriers

In our interviews with nontraditional suppliers, we heard four commonly cited barriers. These were

- a lack of access to and communication from DoD
- an extensive, complex, and inefficient bid and selection process
- administration and management of contracts that created extra work and delays
- a lengthy funding time line and final payments that often also involved delays and gaps.

Lack of Access

The nontraditional suppliers we interviewed noted that though they often had questions when preparing a bid, they either could not get any response from DoD staff or they could not get one that was detailed enough for their needs. This was the case whether the questions were about the bidding process, their qualifications, the project's technical requirements, completed and unsuccessful bids, or DoD program needs in general. Post-award communication was also reportedly a problem.

Bidding Process

The nontraditional suppliers said that fully interpreting RFPs and developing a successful bid required knowing the Federal Acquisition Regulation and federal contracting procedures to the same extent that DoD contracting officers do. Such knowledge takes years to acquire and is thus expensive for a business to develop. Even with the knowledge, suppliers noted that developing a bid could cost anywhere from $25,000 to $1,000,000 and is far more complicated than developing bids for commercial projects or even for state or local governments. They also reported inefficiencies in the federal process, such as having to provide multiple copies of the same extensive background material for each bid.

Administration and Management of Contracts

Our interviewees noted particular problems with contract management by the Defense Contract Management Agency (DCMA) or the Defense Contract Audit Agency (DCAA). Correcting errors, whether by DoD or the contractor, could be extremely difficult, and critical errors affecting the scope of work or payment could take months or even years to fix if contract management had shifted from the original contracting officer to DCMA. Similarly, final contract payments could reportedly be stalled for years because of large DCAA backlogs.

Funding Time Line

The lengthy time between submission of a bid and award of the first payment could be particularly problematic. This was especially true for small and new businesses with less capital to sustain operations to include key personnel. Interviewees also claimed that federal budget processes could lead to funding cancellation even after a contract was awarded, which essentially wasted their scarce bid and proposal funds.

Other Barriers

Other, less frequently cited barriers included DoD web sites used to advertise bidding opportunities that were difficult and time-consuming to navigate, regulations affecting firms wishing to sell internationally, and small business preference programs, which occasionally deterred other-than-small firms from competing.

DoD Perceptions of Common Barriers

We also interviewed DoD small business specialists regarding their perceptions of common barriers to nontraditional suppliers. DoD staff confirmed some of the barriers that nontraditional suppliers reported, including that bidders need to know acquisition processes and regulations just as well as DoD contracting specialists, that obtaining this knowledge is easier for large firms than for small or new ones, and that contracting specialists offer little detail when answering questions because they perceive that the request for proposal includes all necessary information.

Our DoD interviewees' perceptions differed from those of the commercial firms: They firmly insisted that contracting specialists would return inquiries directed to them, whether about a proposal under development or about a failed bid. They also reported that information about award decisions was posted online and that post-award debriefings were guaranteed by the Federal Acquisition Regulation.

Comparison with Prior Reviews of Barriers

Compared with the barriers from previous assessments described above, our interviews confirmed some obstacles, suggested that others may not be as problematic as previously thought, and identified some new ones. The most common barriers identified in previous reviews were confirmed in the present interviews with nontraditional suppliers: the cumbersome and lengthy bidding process and the lack of visibility and communication. To a lesser extent, the interviewees also confirmed facing the barriers of unique cost-accounting procedures, restricted commercial opportunities, funding uncertainty, loss of commercial intellectual property, and inadequate support for the full development of new technology. We did not find evidence of a preference for other-than-small suppliers or any discussion of DoD personnel capabilities. In addition to the barriers identified in earlier reviews, our interviews also identified problems with inefficiencies and duplications in the bidding process, contract management and final payment, an incumbent advantage because of risk-aversion among DoD personnel, and cumbersome web sites.

Conclusions and Recommendations

Our findings point to two sets of recommendations, one that can be implemented immediately and another that addresses deeper problems and will take longer to implement.

Initial Recommendations
Immediate steps include improving communication between DoD and suppliers, both by having contracting officers available to answer questions and by providing more information on substantive requirements. Bidding processes could be streamlined by standardizing the process and reducing the paperwork required for it. Creating a list of prequalified suppliers, including nontraditional ones, could also reduce delays and the number of bids with extremely low chances of winning. Background materials might be stored on a DoD-wide or even federal-wide site and retrieved as necessary for consideration of bidders.

Longer-Term Recommendations
Longer-term steps may include further simplifying and speeding payment processes. Other steps may include reducing backlogs at DCMA and DCAA, noting the chances of project cancellation, and adopting best commercial procurement practices or even those used in state and local governments, which tend to be far less cumbersome.

Acknowledgments

This research would not have been possible without the work of many people. First, we thank the nontraditional supplier companies, DoD contracting staff, and DoD staff engaged in future DoD industrial needs who generously offered their experience to this research, taking time out of their busy schedules to do so. Without these contributions in particular, we would have an incomplete understanding of the barriers facing nontraditional suppliers. We are also deeply grateful to our sponsor, the Office of Small Business Programs at the Department of Defense, for supporting this research. In particular, Andre Gudger, Linda Oliver, Kasey Diaz, and Linda Robinson all contributed to this project. We also thank our reviewers, Susan Gates and Lisa Ellram, for their feedback, which substantially improved this document. Last, we thank our RAND colleagues for insightful comments and capable assistance in bringing this report to fruition: Cynthia Cook, Paul DeLuca, Judy Mele, Patricia Bedrosian, and Donna Mead.

Abbreviations

CCR	Central Contractor Registration
DCAA	Defense Contract Audit Agency
DCMA	Defense Contract Management Agency
DoC	Department of Commerce
DoD	Department of Defense
FAR	Federal Acquisition Regulation
FY	fiscal year
GAO	Government Accountability Office
HASC	House Armed Services Committee
IDIQ	Indefinite Delivery, Indefinite Quantity
ITAR	International Traffic in Arms Regulations
NAF	nonappropriated funds
NAICS	North American Industry Classification System
NDAA	National Defense Authorization Act
ODUSD	Office of the Deputy Under Secretary of Defense
PM	Program Manager
RFP	request for proposal
SBIR	Small Business Innovation Research
U.S.C.	U.S. Code

CHAPTER ONE

Nontraditional Suppliers to the Department of Defense

The Department of Defense (DoD) seeks innovative technologies to help it stay on the cutting edge of warfare and identify new ways to reduce its total costs. Many suppliers with prospective cutting-edge goods and services for DoD may be new to the defense marketplace and may face challenges to successfully entering it.

The possible challenges that nontraditional suppliers may have in contracting with DoD led Congress to request, in the National Defense Authorization Act (NDAA) for fiscal year (FY) 2011, that the Secretary of Defense "review barriers to firms that are not traditional suppliers to the Department of Defense wishing to contract with the Department of Defense and develop a set of recommendations on the elimination of such barriers" (Public Law 111-383, 2011). DoD, in turn, authorized RAND to undertake this review. Our goal in responding to Congress's request is to review what has been found previously about barriers to nontraditional suppliers, augment this with anonymous input from suppliers, and identify any steps Congress and DoD can take to address these barriers.

What Are Nontraditional Suppliers and Why Are They of Concern?

Congress states that "a firm is not a traditional supplier of the Department of Defense if it does not currently have contracts and subcontracts to perform work for the Department of Defense with a total combined value in excess of $500,000" (Public Law 111-383, 2011). We rely primarily on this definition as much as possible in our analysis, but we note that there have been recurring and occasionally varying definitions of such suppliers.[1]

---

[1] Indeed, because of the nature of subcontracting data, it has not been possible to identify all firms receiving at least $500,000 in subcontract awards. Until March 1, 2011, for example, the threshold for reporting data on subcontracts was $550,000, more than that which Congress used to define "nontraditional" suppliers—making it impossible to identify such suppliers in subcontracts.

The $500,000 threshold is perhaps the most common way used to define nontraditional suppliers. U.S. Code (10 U.S.C. 2371) currently defines nontraditional defense contractors, for purposes of awarding research projects other than through contracts or grants, as entities that have not had a contract subject to the Federal Acquisition Regulation for more than $500,000 in the previous year. The Government Accountability Office (GAO) (2004, 2008) used a similar definition for the Department of Homeland Security as well as for "high-technology" firms that might provide "innovative technologies." The Congressional Research Service (Grasso, 2010; Halchin, 2010) has also used similar definitions, while noting that in specified areas the federal government has offered some preferences to self-certified nontraditional suppliers. Some in Congress have sought to restrict any focus on "nontraditional suppliers" to firms having no more than $100,000 in DoD contracts in the previous five years and to industries of concern to those sectors in which DoD spends at least $500 million annually. Many of these industries are precisely those where small businesses may have difficulty gaining DoD contracts for scale or other reasons (Moore et al., 2008).

Nontraditional suppliers are of interest to policymakers for two reasons. First, many in Congress see expansion of the DoD supply base to nontraditional suppliers as a way to "get more competitors involved in the process" of providing goods and services to DoD (Rutherford, 2010). The initiative to find and include more nontraditional contractors in the DoD supply base is part of a broader initiative to improve how the military purchases not only weapon systems but also other goods and services on which it spends more money, and specifically in areas where DoD "is not obtaining good commercial pricing" (Matthews, 2010). Small businesses were of particular concern to recent initiatives. As the chairman of a House Armed Services Committee (HASC) panel on defense-acquisition reform claimed, DoD "can and should better utilize small business to access new innovative technologies and to enhance the discipline that competition brings to acquisition" (Andrews, 2009).

Second, and perhaps more important, policymakers see nontraditional suppliers as the likely locus of innovation for meeting DoD's future needs. As the chairman of a panel on defense-acquisition reform argues:

> Most people intuitively understand that truly revolutionary ideas and technologies almost never come from the dominant firms in an industry . . . we are quite likely to find that the "next big thing" in defense acquisition will be something developed by small firm or a nontraditional defense supplier (Andrews, 2009).

Research Approach

Our central question in this research is, what barriers do nontraditional suppliers face in trying to work for DoD? To answer this question, we completed four principal tasks. First, we reviewed recent efforts by the federal government related to barriers facing nontraditional suppliers.[2] Findings from this review are presented in Chapter Two. Second, we identified industries of particular interest to DoD and in which it may most wish to find new, potentially innovative suppliers, and we sampled firms from those industries for our interviews. This is summarized in Chapter Three. Third, we interviewed nontraditional suppliers and associated DoD staff in the identified industries of particular DoD interest; the results of these interviews are presented in Chapter Four. Finally, we draw together these findings with the findings of prior work to develop recommendations, which we present in Chapter Five.

---

[2]   The House Armed Services Committee (HASC) Panel on Business Challenges in the Defense Industry was established on September 12, 2011, to examine the challenges that businesses face when working with DoD. The panel held hearings and meetings over a six-month period to examine these challenges (HASC Panel on Business Challenges within the Defense Industry, 2012).

CHAPTER TWO

Attracting Nontraditional Suppliers: A Recurring Problem

Interest in including nontraditional suppliers dates back many decades. For nearly the entire history of the military-aircraft industry, key innovations have typically arisen from "second-rank prime contractors, companies either moving into new areas of aircraft specialization or totally new entrants" (Lorell, 2003, p. 117). This, in turn, has periodically raised questions of how to foster innovation when there are a few dominant firms or even only one, and seemingly insurmountable barriers to new entrants,[1] especially in periods of normal technological evolution (Lorell and Levaux, 1998). More broadly in defense industries, the end of the Cold War brought a realization that "to satisfy its future needs, the Pentagon may have to turn to companies that are not currently doing business with it," especially as procurement of weapon systems decreased and purchases of other goods and services increased (Rich, 1990, p. 13).

Congress has sought to broaden the DoD supplier base to include nontraditional suppliers several times, claiming that "DoD's regulatory barriers and its acquisition culture have . . . resulted in higher costs [and] kept commercial products from being used in the defense sector," (Grasso, 2003, p. 1). These have included efforts to simplify government procedures for procuring commercial products as well as to remove other barriers, such as certified cost and pricing data, for acquiring products, and streamlining contracting requirements to promote better communication between the government and potential contract bidders. Nevertheless, suppliers seeking to gain DoD contracts have encountered similar recurring problems in recent years.

In this chapter, we review recent efforts by the U.S. federal government to identify and address barriers facing nontraditional suppliers. These have included a DoD "roadmap" for "transforming the defense industrial base," a 2004 Department of Commerce (DoC) assessment of industry attitudes on collaborating with DoD in research and development, a 2006 GAO forum on managing the DoD supplier base, assessments of policies that pose barriers to DoD's ability to leverage the commercial sector, and a House Armed Services Committee panel on business challenges and ways to address them. We review each of these efforts below and conclude the chapter with a summary of key issues.

---

[1] Porter (1985) outlines the following barriers to entry: economics of scale, proprietary product differences, brand identity, switching costs, capital requirements, access to distribution, absolute cost advantages, proprietary learning curve, access to necessary inputs, proprietary low-cost product design, government policy, and expected retaliation.

The 2003 DoD Roadmap

In 2003, the Office of the Deputy Under Secretary of Defense (ODUSD) (Industrial Policy) published *Transforming the Defense Industrial Base: A Roadmap*. This report was part of an effort to advance earlier DoD transformation goals and to apply those goals to transform DoD's industrial base to garner "the most important, most innovative, and fastest products" (ODUSD, 2003, p. iv). This report identified ways to open opportunities for emerging defense suppliers and identified six areas of concern for new entrants to the defense supplier base.

First, emerging suppliers did not understand military contracting processes or how best to make initial contact. They claimed to have "insufficient visibility into the military enterprise" (ODUSD, 2003, p. 22). One who also lamented the difficulties of being outside the "defense beltway" said, "If I wanted to crack General Motors, I could find a plant site. . . . If I show up [at a local base], they don't let me in the gate. I just don't know where to start" (ODUSD, 2003, p. B-71) That much of DoD's buying is localized only exacerbates this barrier; suppliers would need to identify which base or bases are relevant in addition to having a contact on the base.

Second, emerging suppliers saw few ways to bridge the gap between the basic research needed for initial development of technology and that to field the developed technology. They claimed that there was "inadequate funding and advocacy for new technology transition" (ODUSD, 2003, p. 22). Similar problems have been evident in the Small Business Innovation Research (SBIR) program (Held et al., 2006). Few companies, especially among small, emerging, or nontraditional suppliers, have the means to fund technology transitions, particularly for military products. Indeed, the difficulties of attracting funding after initial research but before prototype can be so great that many refer to this period as the "valley of death."

Third, emerging suppliers have found it difficult to build relationships with defense and related customers (ODUSD, 2003). A representative of one noted the need for "a high level champion" in getting any contact within DoD able to recognize the value of an innovative technology and willing to guide it through the bureaucratic hurdles that must be overcome for funding (ODUSD, 2003, p. B-106).[2] Others suggested that DoD requests for proposals focus on broad systems (e.g., weapon systems) rather than on smaller, innovative solutions, which make it more difficult for small firms to bid.[3] Offering innovative products to large DoD prime contractors is one way in which some new suppliers can enter the defense supply base, but others have found it difficult and even "ended up getting ripped off" (ODUSD, 2003, p. B-5). The need for security clearances also affected the relationships that emerging suppliers were able to build with DoD. In one unique case, a firm refused to acquire a clearance for its chief scientist, fearing that this could stifle creativity for other customers. The increasingly global nature of innovative technology has caused some concerns for emerging suppliers working with the Pentagon, especially given the controls that the federal government seeks to place on

---

[2]   Recent earmark rules in the House of Representatives are likely to make it more difficult to direct funds to specific companies (Lichtblau, 2010).

[3]   In the 1990s, DoD shifted from breaking out certain weapon system subsystems for direct contract to a lead system integrator approach that outsourced most of a weapon system's supplier relationships to original equipment manufacturers/assemblers.

technology.[4] This can lead to fears among innovative firms that doing business with DoD will limit their ability to do business elsewhere (Tiron, 2006).

Fourth, emerging suppliers have found it difficult to work with the "cumbersome system design specifications" of DoD (ODUSD, 2003, p. 22). The assumed DoD preference noted above for seeking broad systems rather than smaller, innovative solutions restricts the ability of emerging suppliers to specify innovative and varied solutions to achieve a mission. Emerging suppliers also perceived DoD as highly risk-averse and therefore not a likely customer for them; several noted "nobody ever got fired for choosing" a large, well-known prime contractor (ODUSD, 2003, p. B-6). Emerging suppliers also complained of burdensome DoD contracting and accounting procedures and the need to create a bureaucracy they could not support to manage federal government reporting requirements.

Fifth, emerging suppliers complained of sales cycles that were difficult to manage because of their length and complexity (ODUSD, 2003). One contrasted in particular "the ability (and preference) of its commercial customers to clearly state their technology needs upfront, quickly evaluate . . . products, and promptly finalize purchase decisions," with its military sales, which had a "'start-and-stop' pattern" that led it to focus on "commercial applications or else we wo[uld]n't survive" (ODUSD, 2003, p. B-95).

Sixth, emerging suppliers claimed to lack the capital needed to develop products for one likely customer, DoD. They described "limited access to development and investment capital" for defense work (ODUSD, 2003, p. 22). For example, one producer of antidotes for anthrax and other "bio-warfare agents" faced difficulties because large pharmaceutical companies and venture capitalists had little interest in the bio-warfare market. Their lack of interest stemmed from its limited commercial potential as well as from military agencies that were uncoordinated or slow in contracting and that worked only with one-year commitments. This same supplier claimed that it also generally preferred commercial markets because they were far more able to devise and follow a testing milestone program. Another supplier, which produced sensory equipment in high demand from the military following the attacks on the *USS Cole* in October 2000 and again after the terrorist attacks against the United States in September 2001, found no opportunity to develop its products between the two attacks in part because of a "military acquisition attitude and outlook [that] is highly risk-averse" as well as the lack of a "well-defined funding source . . . to support technologies past initial stage research through pre-production" (ODUSD, 2003, pp. B-23, B-25) Emerging suppliers also noted difficulties in accessing DoD capital for developing innovative technologies.

Forum on Industry Attitudes

Similar issues emerged when the Air Force commissioned an assessment of industry attitudes on collaborating with DoD in research and development and in sharing technology (DoC, 2004). Specifically, nondefense suppliers found the commercial marketplace easier to navigate than the public sector generally and the military in particular, and focused their efforts accordingly. Small firms not currently contracting with DoD considered their size to be an impedi-

---

[4] International Traffic in Arms Regulation (ITAR) (U.S. Department of State, 2011) controls the export and import of defense-related articles and services. Enterprises that transfer such articles and services to unauthorized parties face large fines.

ment. Other nondefense suppliers feared loss of proprietary data, limited economic benefit, and reduced competitive advantage by contracting with the military. Lack of communication and information regarding public opportunities and contract procedures was cited by nondefense suppliers as the biggest impediment to entering the military market. Procurement complexity was also considered to be so great as to not only dissuade nondefense suppliers from entering the military market but even to force some defense suppliers to exit the field.

Managing Supplier Bases to Include Nontraditional Suppliers

A forum sponsored by the GAO (2006) identified still more similar concerns and possible ways to address them. This forum was convened specifically to address acquisition challenges faced by DoD and other federal agencies, including changes to security threats, science and technology, procurement responsibility, the organization of industry, and decreases in program budgets and acquisition staff. Participants noted the concern that "small innovative businesses and other suppliers" had for such perceived risks as fixed profit margins, uncertain funding, and the difficulties in navigating the federal acquisition marketplace (GAO, 2006, summary page). The forum also noted the difficulties that innovative technology firms had in adopting limits to profit margins, cost-accounting standards, and other requirements that traditional DoD prime contractors follow.

Proposed solutions included developing a flexible acquisition strategy for innovative products and services (e.g., allowing higher profits to companies pursuing technologies that are riskier to develop); targeting investments, particularly in small companies, into needed emerging technologies; increasing government visibility of lower-tier suppliers and decreasing barriers for such firms to access government contracts; and employing acquisition strategies that promote innovation rather than risk-averse approaches. Participants also noted the difficulties resulting from a DoD inability to differentiate between mature technology markets, where new suppliers might not be expected to emerge, and those where emerging suppliers might be more prevalent.

Policies That Pose Barriers to DoD's Leveraging of the Commercial Sector

Many current policies are barriers to DoD's leveraging of the commercial sector. Two other efforts, a book on the defense industry (Gansler, 2011) and a plan by the Office of the Under Secretary of Defense for Acquisition, Technology, and Logistics (2008) raise these issues. For example, government-imposed business practices often lead commercial sector firms to create separate, defense-unique organizations and facilities for any defense goods and services they produce. This increases costs and limits the ability of firms to leverage commercial innovations. Further, "many technology-rich companies (such as Hewlett Packard, 3M, and Corning) declined to participate in critical [DoD] research and development projects" because of complex government rules, such as those requiring highly specialized cost accounting practices, and the need to ensure that subcontractors also adhere to contractual and other regulations unique to DoD (Gansler, 2011, p. 34). Leading commercial firms also had concerns about proprietary rights and viewed the defense business as unattractive because of relatively low profits and excessive regulation, particularly when defense budgets are shrinking.

Other barriers to attracting nontraditional firms include special-interest legislative rules prohibiting the purchase of some items from foreign sources, such as the Berry Amendment to the Buy American Act (1933), which originally "requires 100 percent of the goods in three categories (food, textiles, and tools) to be domestically produced, manufactured, or home grown" and was "incrementally expanded" and "in the early 1970s it included 'specialty metals'" used in diverse products such as flatware, electronic components,[5] and jet engines (Gansler, 2011, p. 73). After the terrorist attacks of September 11, 2001, restrictions on using non-U.S. citizens for defense-related research and production as well as on exports of U.S. technology increased significantly. This further raised barriers to the DoD market for nontraditional firms with foreign workers and markets. Last, government procurement regulations and restrictions, which had been simplified in the early 1990s specifically to attract more nontraditional firms, increased significantly after the discovery of numerous fraud, waste, and abuse cases and high-profile corruption scandals resulting from significant increases in spending to support operations in Iraq and Afghanistan. These lengthened defense-procurement processes and discouraged risk-taking by procurement personnel and officials, which further discouraged nontraditional firms from bidding on DoD offers, perceiving that their chances of success had diminished and that the likelihood of increased time from bid to award, or worse, cancellation of the offer, had increased.

A general plan by the Office of the Under Secretary of Defense for Acquisition, Technology, and Logistics (2008) to create a more effective defense industrial policy reiterated yet again several proposals that, conceivably, could help nontraditional suppliers enter the military marketplace. These included being able to manage technology-procurement cycles measured "in months rather than years," achieving "greater visibility" into the capabilities of nontraditional suppliers, and changing specialized cost-accounting standards for nontraditional suppliers (Office of the Under Secretary of Defense for Acquisition, Technology, and Logistics, 2008, pp. 4, 29).

Recurring Issues

Despite these repeated efforts, many longstanding concerns continue to recur. Nontraditional firms continue to have difficulties understanding the defense-acquisition process, rules, and regulations and to retain concerns over technology transfer (Greenwalt, 2009).

Small firms that policymakers think most innovative continue to find it difficult to weather program delays and the intermittent nature of defense procurement (Butler, 2011). Defense officials also fear that acquisition by large defense suppliers of smaller firms can eliminate the "innovative culture" of the smaller firms (Butler, 2011, p. 24).

Finally, many small firms, having no interest in creating the bureaucracy they think necessary for government work, avoid DoD contracts altogether (Erwin, 2011).[6] Indeed, as one industry analyst contends, the bureaucracy necessary to support "plodding" government pro-

---

[5]   "Fortunately, the 2007 Defense Authorization Act did exclude commercial electronic components from the Berry Amendment" (Gansler, 2011, p. 74).

[6]   For example, the Office of Management and Budget (2013) sets the benchmark compensation amount allowable under government contracts for certain executives. The amount for contractors' in FY 2011 was set at $763,029.

grams will dissuade firms who must compete for engineers who may not wish to work "on a project that's going to require four bureaucrats for every one engineer" (Erwin, 2011).

House Armed Services Committee Panel on Business Challenges

One of the most recent efforts to address concerns of nontraditional suppliers was a panel convened in September 2011 by the HASC on Business Challenges in the Defense Industry. The panel held seven hearings, conducted eight industry roundtables at different locations, and received two briefings, summarizing its findings and recommendations in a March 2012 report (HASC Panel on Business Challenges in the Defense Industry, 2012).

Barriers that participants noted to the panel included

- inadequate communication of DoD needs, requirements, and changes
- poor access to DoD customers and program offices, particularly for small subcontractors
- complex, slow, bureaucratic, variable, inadequate (e.g., in market research), and costly DoD processes
- adversarial, unresponsive, unaccountable, inefficient, and burdensome DoD agencies
- slow and underfunded technology research, development, and transfer
- few or no incentives for innovation in quality, performance, or technology, given preference for low-price, technically acceptable bids
- perception that DoD and prime contractors prefer other-than-small contractors
- inadequate protection of intellectual property and proprietary data
- inconsistent or inadequate training, capabilities, and incentives for changing DoD personnel
- regulations limiting the sale of goods (e.g,. ITAR).

Business participants also expressed concern over the closing of one possible way to bridge funding from initial research to a prototype that is able to attract commercial research. Specifically, business owners were concerned that, "with the elimination of earmarks, more innovative technologies will have a tougher time getting across the 'valley of death'" (HASC Panel on Business Challenges in the Defense Industry, 2012, p. 92).

To overcome these barriers, the HASC panel made several recommendations, including

- developing policies, mechanisms, and organizational structures to improve industry communications, oversight, and management
- developing business processes and information technology to track subcontractor work and performance, support market research, and identify critical industrial-base issues
- providing incentives to DoD personnel and contractors to meet small-business goals
- improving methods for setting small business size standards
- improving the defense program management and acquisition workforce
- simplifying acquisition, review, audit, and technology-transition processes and funding
- developing measures of effectiveness and performance for acquisition programs regarding their success at leveraging technology developed by small businesses
- repealing or amending outdated regulations with unintended consequences

- assessing how well DoD complies with current law and policy on the use, disclosure, and release of intellectual property
- reducing the backlog and improving the performance and coordination of audits as well as the relationship between audit agencies and the industrial base.

Summary of Recurring Problems in Attracting Nontraditional Suppliers

Previous analyses have noted myriad barriers to nontraditional suppliers seeking DoD contracts, and several appear to be recurring. Many of these problems may be inherent in the government-contracting process, unintended side effects of a process that values inclusive and open competition, transparency, and prevention of all fraud and abuse over all other issues. Conversely, streamlining processes to eliminate these problems and attract nontraditional suppliers might inadvertently and adversely affect other government goals in contracting.

Table 2.1 summarizes the most significant barriers to nontraditional suppliers identified in similar past efforts and the principal sources for our discussion of these. We also discuss each briefly below.

Perhaps the most prevalent concern over time has been the federal government's *cumbersome and lengthy bid-and-selection processes*. These have included cumbersome design specifications, greater difficulties navigating DoD than commercial markets, increasing regulations that effectively lengthen the bid-and-selection processes, and other bureaucratic complexities. Many have noted that these processes require specialized units or employees. *Unique cost-accounting procedures* can be among the specific DoD processes that nontraditional suppliers find cumbersome. The need to create separate facilities for defense goods for unique requirements can increase costs and limit the ability of nontraditional suppliers to innovate at a reasonable cost.

Table 2.1
Summary of Past Discussions on Barriers

Barrier	Source of Discussion				
	ODUSD (2003)	DoC (2004)	GAO (2006)	Gansler (2011)	HASC (2012)
Cumbersome and lengthy bid-and-selection processes requiring specialized knowledge and staff	X	X		X	X
Lack of visibility, communication, or information, particularly for design specifications	X	X	X		X
Unique cost-accounting procedures			X	X	
Restricted or limited commercial opportunities (including international)	X	X		X	
Funding uncertainty			X		
Loss of intellectual property or proprietary data		X		X	X
Inadequate support for developing new technology	X				X
Perceived DoD preference for large suppliers	X				X
DoD personnel capabilities					X

Another recurring theme, the *lack of visibility, communication, or information*, can make it difficult to navigate the DoD marketplace. Design specifications came up in this context too, with suppliers having compared DoD specification processes unfavorably with those of commercial buyers. Suppliers have also complained about lack of access points into DoD.[7]

Many of these processes compound or are compounded by other barriers as well, contributing to an opaqueness of DoD.

The nature of DoD purchases also *restricted or limited commercial opportunities* for firms. Many products that DoD seeks have little or no commercial market. When combined with the *funding uncertainty* around federal budgets and defense demand, including possible project cancellation, companies can face strong limits on the returns to DoD investments. Controls that the Department of State places on international sales of emerging technologies further limits profitability and may also dissuade firms from seeking to develop a global market from developing products for the military.

Companies may also have concerns about a *loss of intellectual property or proprietary data*. They have criticized an inadequate protection of intellectual property and proprietary data, with some companies complaining of "getting ripped off" when offering innovative ideas (ODUSD, 2003, p. B-5).

Some companies willing to offer innovative ideas or technology to DoD have claimed that there is *inadequate support for developing new technology*. This is a particularly acute need when crossing the "valley of death" between initial research and prototype development.

Nontraditional suppliers in the past have also *perceived a DoD preference for larger suppliers*. One reason cited for this is military aversion to risk.

Finally, the HASC hearings suggested that *DoD personnel capabilities* may need to improve for nontraditional suppliers to participate in requests for proposals (RFPs). Better-trained personnel with more incentives for innovation could help bring more nontraditional firms into the DoD supply base.

Despite these reviews of barriers to nontraditional DoD suppliers, Congress asked for a new analysis in the 2011 NDAA. Our goal in responding to Congress's request is to combine these earlier reviews with new information from suppliers and clarify what steps Congress and DoD can take to address these barriers. Our interviews with nontraditional suppliers, described in the chapters that follow, drew on these previous reviews and sought new information by providing a forum in which suppliers could speak anonymously.

The history of barriers facing nontraditional suppliers to DoD also raises several questions. First, what is the status of these barriers; do they continue to persist? Second, if they do persist, are they intractable or can DoD take actions to address them and thereby expand its supply base? Third, do nontraditional suppliers face new or additional barriers regarding entry into the military marketplace? To better focus our discussion of these questions, we turn next to consideration of the industries of greatest concern to DoD for accessing nontraditional suppliers.

---

[7]   This is not a problem unique to DoD. Small businesses also "find it particularly challenging to locate the right representatives at larger companies (Horn and Pleasance, 2012).

CHAPTER THREE

Industries of Greatest Interest to the Department of Defense

Because technology innovation, particularly for future warfare, is among the chief reasons DoD seeks nontraditional suppliers, we wanted to focus our interviews with such suppliers in innovative industries of most interest to DoD. We used the Central Contractor Registration (CCR)[1] to identify these firms. The CCR indicates the willingness of a firm to do business with the federal government, which is prohibited from contracting with firms not in the CCR, except under certain circumstances, such as local support for overseas operations and for nation-building purposes. Firms in the CCR identify the industries within which they believe they are qualified to provide goods and services using North American Industry Classification System (NAICS) codes.[2] A firm may list as many as 1,000 six-digit NAICS codes in the CCR.

To identify industries of most interest to DoD, we searched for recent reports, briefings, and web pages outlining technologies sought by DoD or the military services. Specifically, we

1. asked the DoD Office of Industrial Policy for industries of priority to it, but learned it had no prioritized list, particularly by NAICS code
2. searched literature and DoD web pages on future DoD technology and industry priorities
3. reviewed reports, briefings, and web pages to identify future technology reports; unfortunately, few of these sources related priorities to specific industries and those reports that did identify industries listed a very broad range of primary industries for firms that provided the technology, but there was no good correlation in these sources between technologies and NAICS codes
4. assigned NAICS codes that appeared closest to the future technology interest when no NAICS code was given for it
5. listed all NAICS codes linked to technologies for each source

---

[1] After this study was completed, the CCR transitioned on July 30, 2012, to the System for Award Management.

[2] The Office of Management and Budget Economic Classification Policy Committee, which comprises representatives from the Bureau of Economic Analysis, the Bureau of Labor Statistics, and the Census Bureau, is responsible for creating and maintaining the NAICS, which are reviewed and revised every five years before the Economic Census. The Economic Census, which surveys businesses every five years, produces statistics by NAICS code. NAICS codes are typically from two to six digits, with two-digit codes identifying broad sectors, four-digit codes identifying subsectors, and six-digit codes identifying specific industries. For example, 54 is the two-digit code for firms providing Professional, Scientific, and Technical Services, 5415 is the four-digit code for firms providing Computer Systems Design and Related Services, and 541511 is the six-digit code for firms providing Custom Computer Programming Services. For more information, see U.S. Department of Commerce (2012).

6. input the NAICS code for the future technology interest in each source into a spread-sheet (see Appendix A for a table linking NAICS codes to future DoD technologies of interest)
7. tallied the number of reports associated with each NAICS code
8. identified the NAICS codes associated with the most reports on future technology interests.

We reviewed this process with our sponsor and invited discussion on it.

Using this process, we selected three industries for further research, one each from man-ufacturing, services, and research and development industries. These were

- 334511—Search, Detection, Navigation, Guidance, Aeronautical, and Nautical System and Instrument Manufacturing
- 541511—Custom Computer Programming Services
- 541712—Research and Development in the Physical, Engineering, and Life Sciences (except Biotechnology)

These industries appeared in reports in 2003 and/or 2004 as well as in more recent reports in 2010 and/or 2011. The fact that they appeared in reports by different DoD organizations over the past six to eight years suggests that they are of relatively broad as well as recent inter-est. Focusing on these three should provide timely insights that are more likely to apply across DoD.

Sampling Methodology

Once we identified several industries that develop innovative technologies of interest to DoD, we developed a protocol of questions to ask companies in those industries and a plan for sampling which companies to interview and which DoD staff to interview. We based our interview questions on potential barriers identified in the literature, policies, and Congres-sional hearings. Ideally, we would have asked about each of these potential barriers individu-ally, but this would have resulted in interviews that were many hours long and too great a burden for our interviewees. Previous experience in asking commercial contractors to partici-pate in a federal study indicated to us that few if any firms would participate in such a long interview. Similarly, previous experience in interviewing DoD staff indicated that they also would not have the time to devote to such a long interview. Therefore, we organized and priori-tized the list of barriers into broad areas. We asked about these general barriers in an interview that could be completed in 30 to 40 minutes. We included prompts for individual barriers that we could ask about when time permitted. The resulting protocols thus balanced the substantive needs of the study with the time constraints of those being interviewed. (See Appendix B for our business and DoD staff interview protocols.)

We also had to address the potential concerns of the nontraditional suppliers that criti-cisms of DoD processes might jeopardize their chances of winning a DoD contract. To do so, we assured companies in our initial contacts and during the interviews that we would not identify any person or company we interviewed by name, nor would we share any specific information that could identify them. Rather, we would aggregate our findings and share the results in general ways that described common barriers faced by all nontraditional suppliers.

For our company interviews, we used a stratified random sample to assure that we had a broad cross-section of companies in the three key industries we identified as being of interest to DoD. In particular, we sampled firms that were registered in one of the three industries or that had obtained funding in one of the industries even if only registered in other NAICS. Although not all nontraditional suppliers are in the CCR, DoD's first step in expanding its supply base should be to include firms that have indicated their willingness to do business with it by registering in the CCR but to date have done little business with it. Investigating barriers to firms that may be willing to do business with DoD but have not registered in the CCR is a second layer of study and is beyond the scope of the present analysis, a point with which our project sponsor concurred. Although some of these firms may be very innovative, they may have no interest in working with DoD or may be interested but lack the willingness or capacity to complete DoD contracting requirements. Therefore, we defined nontraditional suppliers as companies registered in the CCR that had less than $500,000 in prime contracts (including subsidiaries of the same parent company) with DoD in 2011 (per the NDAA).[3]

To obtain a cross-section of the amount of business a firm did in the three industries, we stratified our sample of firms registered in the three NAICS, as shown in Table 3.1. We randomly sampled up to eight companies in each of the eight groups shown. For example, row one refers to companies that registered in all three of the key industries and that had DoD contracts in these industries only; row two refers to companies that registered in two of the three key industries and that had DoD contracts only in those in which they registered. The last three rows refer to companies with contracts in industries other than the three on which we focused. This yielded 141 companies that we contacted for interviews. Most (85 percent) were considered small in at least one of the three industries. That only 16 of the companies responded to our interview requests means that although the sampling frame is representative of all firms in these industries, we cannot claim that the interviewed firms are equally representative. At the same time, as we describe below, the substantial overlap in their responses is an indicator of their shared experience.

Table 3.1
Sampling Firms to Interview

Industry Registration	DoD Contracts
All 3 industries	All in these industries
2 industries	All in these 2 industries
2 industries	All in 1 of these 2 industries
1 industry	All in this 1 industry
1–3 industries	Most in these industries
1–3 industries	Less than half in these industries
1–3 industries	None in the 3 industries

---

[3] Our analyses to select these firms exclude procurements from nonappropriated funds (NAF). Given that NAF procurement is associated with morale, welfare, and recreation activities and that fees from one activity are used to subsidize others, we doubt that this substantially affects our findings.

We identified a large number of firms to interview because previous experience with soliciting private firms for government research indicated that we would likely obtain a low response rate. We sent numerous follow-up contacts to increase the number of firms responding. Of the 141 firms contacted, 16 responded after one or more requests to participate. The 16 companies we interviewed represented a wide range of the characteristics on which we sampled and, as shown in Table 3.2, looked quite similar to the carefully selected sample. The interviewed firms had a comparable amount of DoD funding, whether measured for the specific contractor or for its parent company (if the company was a subsidiary of a larger corporate group). The interviewed firms had more employees than the firms in the sample, on average, although the range of employees was similar, and the annual receipts for the two groups were similar as well, in both average and range. In addition to the characteristics in Table 3.2, all of the firms interviewed were registered in one or more of the three key industries; 15 had at least one contract in one of those three industries; 15 had bid for contracts that they did not win; 15 had been a subcontractor on another firm's contract; and 10 were certified small businesses in at least some industries. Across this variation, and given the similarity between the interviewed firms and the broader sample, the several common themes heard in the interview responses give us confidence that we have identified the barriers that are most salient to nontraditional suppliers.

To obtain the sample of DoD staff, we used the Federal Procurement Data System to generate a list of all contracts received by the firms we interviewed and any information about the contracting office that was included in the data. We identified the small business specialist and any other staff members who appeared to work with the industrial community in these offices to contact for interviews (e.g., competition advocates). This resulted in 19 DoD staff whom we then contacted for interviews. We purposely did not talk to the contracting officers connected

Table 3.2
Characteristics of Firms Sampled and Firms Interviewed

	Contractors Sampled	Contractors Interviewed
Contract amount – contractor		
Median	136,000	149,725
Mean	186,114	215,082
Range	0–497,806	2,501–488,482
Contract amount – parent		
Median	137,459	149,725
Mean	187,015	215,082
Range	0–497,806	2,501–488,482
Annual revenue		
Median	1,200,000	1,500,000
Range	0–362,822,000	0–362,822,000
Number of employees		
Mean	52	109
Range	0–1,400	0–1,029

to any of the suppliers we interviewed to avoid the possibility of identifying or misidentifying a supplier as one interviewed for this study—suppliers to whom we had assured confidentiality. We sought out small business representatives and other staff responsible for reaching out to small and nontraditional firms to ensure that we learned about efforts to bring nontraditional suppliers into the DoD industrial base.

Of the 19 DoD staff we contacted, only three responded to our repeated requests for participation in the study. There are two likely possibilities for this low response rate. First, the staff members themselves are extremely busy. We have heard this when interviewing DoD contracting staff on other research projects, and the issue may be exacerbated by the time of year in which we contacted the staff members (summer), because more are on vacation as well as busy processing the end-of-year surge in contract spending. Second, staff members may simply not engage in external communication with organizations outside DoD, including those conducting research. Our nontraditional-supplier interviewees also reported difficulties in getting DoD staff to communicate with them.

The three responses we did receive were small business specialists from different military services. They had between five and ten years of experience with DoD procurement in general and experience working with nontraditional suppliers in particular. This experience indicates that they were well versed in barriers facing nontraditional suppliers, and their responses bore this out. Nonetheless, the fact that we have only three voices from DoD means that we may be missing aspects of the DoD staff perspective.

For both our supplier and DoD interviews, the interviews lasted 30 to 60 minutes each and were conducted on the telephone with two research staff. Both staff members shared in note-taking and asking questions, although one focused more on note-taking to increase the detail captured, while the other focused more on asking the questions to maximize clarity in the conversation.

We compiled our results and analyzed them together. First, we examined the responses across each question, noting common barriers and themes. We then examined these barriers and themes to identify commonalities across the questions. We then reexamined interviews that did not fit the most common themes to identify possible reasons for different responses in those interviews. This cross-checking both minimizes the chance of overstating conclusions and provides further insight into the barriers.

CHAPTER FOUR

Interview Results

Our interviews with nontraditional suppliers revealed four frequently stated barriers to working with DoD, as well as several other barriers that companies reported less frequently.

Our protocol showed that the four most commonly stated barriers were

- a lack of access to and communication from DoD—paralleling previously expressed concerns about lack of visibility, communication, or information in DoD contracting policies
- an extensive, complex, and inefficient bidding process—paralleling previously expressed concerns about cumbersome and lengthy bid-and-selection processes
- administration and management of contracts that created extra work and delays—paralleling previously expressed concerns about DoD processes requiring specialized units or employees and unique cost-accounting procedures
- a lengthy funding time line that often also involved delays and gaps—paralleling previously expressed concerns about inadequate support for developing new technology and funding uncertainty.

We review below each of these four barriers that deter firms from bidding on DoD contracts. We also discuss additional concerns that our interviewees raised.

Lack of Access to and Communication from DoD

The most commonly heard barrier to nontraditional suppliers was a lack of access to and responsiveness from DoD. Firms had questions about the bidding process, about their own qualifications, about the technical requirements of RFPs, about unsuccessful bids, and about DoD program needs in general. For each of these sets of questions, most either could not get a response at all or could not get one that was detailed enough for their needs. As one interviewee stated, "My biggest complaint would be you cannot talk to anybody; you cannot talk to a contracting officer. You can call them ten times, you can email them five times; you cannot talk to anyone. Ever." Similarly, several firms reported that when they did get responses, they were often vague, general, or circular; for example, a question about an RFP was referred back to the RFP for the answer.

Technical questions were particularly frustrating for bidders because they wanted to be able to ensure that they were addressing all of the needs of the customer and that they were qualified to do so. However, the RFPs and the answers that they did receive in response to technical questions were often too general for develop an appropriately detailed bid.

One interviewee described this process as like trying to respond to an RFP for a car with four wheels and a gasoline engine, but, after the contract was awarded to another firm, receiving an explanation that the bidder had proposed a car that was brown instead of blue (despite the fact that the RFP had omitted this and many other specifications).

Post-award communication was also reportedly a problem. Many firms did not know if award decisions were announced, when and where the announcements were posted, or, if they did not win, how to get information about how their proposal fared. Interviewees also stated that their requests for this information went unheeded by contracting officials. Whereas nontraditional suppliers in past analyses noted difficulties in finding initial points of contact, those we interviewed noted these difficulties as well in finding follow-up points of contact, which are essential for improving future bids.

Extensive, Complex, and Inefficient Bidding Process

The second most-frequent barrier that business owners reported was a costly, extensive, complex, and inefficient bidding process. Business owners said that fully interpreting an RFP and developing a successful bid required knowing the Federal Acquisition Regulation (FAR) and federal contracting procedures to the same extent that DoD contracting officers do. Such knowledge takes years to acquire and is thus expensive for a business to develop. Many firms were deterred from acquiring this knowledge, given the low rate of winning DoD contracts. Many small businesses cannot afford to obtain all of the specialized knowledge needed to bid successfully. As noted above, firms in past analyses seeking to learn why nontraditional suppliers may not seek DoD business also noted the difficulties in developing specialized units or employees for administering government contracts, which entails incurring costs that smaller firms in particular may not be able to afford.

Related to the extensive regulations are the sizes of the RFP and associated bid, which are both many times larger than those in the private sector or even those for state and local government contracts. For example, one interviewee reported that a bid for the state of California was typically one-third the size of a bid for DoD. This results in bid and proposal costs estimates that can range from $25,000 to $1,000,000. Our interviewees also estimated that obtaining DoD contracts could require 10 to 500 percent more resources than commercial contracts do.

Finally, the work of the DoD bidding process was extensive and costly partly because of inefficiencies built into the process. These included background material that had to be produced for every bid, even though it remained the same from bid to bid (e.g., employee resumes, company boilerplate).

Administration and Management of Contracts

The third most frequently cited barrier was problematic contract management by the Defense Contract Management Agency (DCMA) or the Defense Contract Audit Agency (DCAA). Some companies claimed that DCMA and DCAA made executing contracts and getting paid difficult sometimes. Correcting any error made when the contract was written, whether made by the bidder or by DoD, was extremely difficult. Critical errors affecting the scope of work or payment could take months or even years to correct if contract management had shifted from the original contracting officer to DCMA. Similarly, distribution of final contract funds could be held up for years because of large DCAA backlogs. Although these funds were a relatively small percentage of the contract award, they could still be very important to the budget of a small business. Finally, the large volume of work faced by DoD contracting staff, as well as turnover in contract management, sometimes meant lengthy delays or inconsistent answers to questions. Such concerns paralleled those of suppliers in earlier analyses who noted concerns about DoD processes requiring specialized units or employees and unique accounting procedures and also those who expressed concerns about DoD personnel capabilities.

Lengthy Funding Time Line

The fourth most frequently heard barrier was time lines for bidding and for funding that could deter future work. The lengthy time between submission of a bid and award of the first payment could be particularly problematic. The funding gap between Phase 1 and Phase 2 of SBIR projects was frequently mentioned as one example of this problem (though not the only one). This parallels previously expressed concerns about inadequate support for developing new technology, particularly in the "valley of death" between funding for initial research and that for developing prototypes.

More generally, our interviewees noted, the time between submission and award can be particularly problematic for small and new businesses with less capital to sustain salaries and company operations. Time line delays can also contribute to obsolescence. Sudden ends to delays could also pose problems; insufficient communication with the contractor led to funding with little warning, before the firm was ready. Finally, the federal budget process sometimes led to funding cancellation, even after a contract was awarded. Although this is not supposed to happen after a contract is awarded, we did hear multiple examples of it happening among the firms we interviewed.

Other Barriers Cited by Interviewees

The business owners described other barriers as well, though less frequently than the four mentioned above (i.e., less than half the time). Many of these were unique to our interviews and do not appear to have been cited in past analyses of barriers that nontraditional suppliers faced.

Among the additional barriers our interviewees cited were experience and perception that prior successful DoD experience informally helped win a bid—and hence was a barrier to companies lacking such experience. This was because knowledge of a company's performance and capability from past contracts lowers the risk for customers and contractors, especially if that prior experience was with the same DoD office. Incumbents with good performance reportedly were well suited to win a repeat contract. Some business owners described RFPs that seemed to be written for a specific contractor.

A few owners described rigid timekeeping and accounting requirements that were unique to DoD and that therefore added to their cost of doing business. As noted above, unique cost-accounting procedures have in the past been considered a barrier to nontraditional suppliers. Our interviewees reported that even minor errors resulted in payment delays. Some said that the DoD Wide Area Work Flow[1] system contained errors that also led to delays; others said that the system worked well.

Some interviewees reported that their technical data or ideas were publically distributed during the bidding process; questions they asked were shared with all bidders or their work as an incumbent was included in an RFP. This was more common among firms that had bid on several SBIR grants. Loss of intellectual property or proprietary data, as noted above, has been a repeated concern of nontraditional suppliers in dealing with DoD.

Other barriers, infrequently cited by our interviewees, included DoD web sites used to advertise bidding opportunities that were difficult and time-consuming to navigate. A few firms also said that ITAR deterred them because they have products they may want to sell internationally. This parallels concerns noted above: Nontraditional suppliers' commercial and international opportunities have been restricted or limited because of their military work. Finally, small business preference programs may occasionally deter firms without such preferences from competing, though only one firm mentioned this.

DoD Staff Responses

Our responses from DoD staff confirmed some of the barriers that nontraditional suppliers reported. These included, first, that bidders need to know the Federal Acquisition Regulation as well as a DoD contracting specialist and that they need to know the ins and outs of the DoD bidding process. As the company owners had described, the DoD staff said that knowledge of the FAR and the DoD bidding process is very different from knowledge of commercial business practices, and they acknowledged that the onus to gain that knowledge is entirely on the supplier. They also acknowledged that obtaining this knowledge is easier for large firms with more resources than small or new ones, and they recommended that firms team up with other companies to learn the process. Their perception was that learning the FAR and the bidding process takes continued hard work over a long period of time but that eventually the work would pay off in contracts. One staff member said, "The small guys want to get in quickly, and it's not a quick process."

Another barrier that was also recognized by DoD staff was the limited detail offered by contracting specialists when answering questions. Because they perceive that the RFP includes all necessary information, they often refer bidders back to the RFP to find the answer to their questions. It is not clear whether the RFP does actually include this information (whether the bidder does not understand the process or the FAR sufficiently to find the answer) or whether the RFP lacks sufficient detail to develop a successful bid (or whether the contracting specialist does not understand the technical requirements enough to realize that a technical answer is not in the RFP).

DoD staff also described a barrier or misperception faced by nontraditional suppliers: an expectation that competition is lower than it really is. For example, nontraditional suppliers do not always understand that winning a multiaward contract means that a firm can compete for a task order, not that it will necessarily win one. DoD staff also described heavy competition for small businesses in certain industries that already had many small businesses and, further, small firms' lack of knowledge about this high level of competition.

---

[1] A secure, web-based system for electronic invoicing, receipt, and acceptance (Wide Area Workflow, undated).

Finally, DoD staff reported some different perceptions from nontraditional suppliers about barriers to working with DoD. Both DoD interviewees firmly insisted that the point of contact on an RFP (i.e., the contracting specialist) would return inquiries directed to them. In the event that contracting staff were away from the office for some time (e.g., at a training session), one interviewee recommended that bidders contact the small business office on base for assistance in reaching a different person in the office. Both DoD interviewees also reported that information about award decisions was posted online and that post-award debriefings were guaranteed by the FAR and would be granted if requested within the specified time frame.

The reporting of award decisions and post-award debriefings is representative in many ways of the discrepancy that sometimes exists between how nontraditional suppliers and contracting staff experience the bidding process. First, DoD staff quote the FAR, whereas the suppliers are often in the process of learning the FAR. Second, the suppliers must find the information they need and request any service they need on their own. Third, there seems to be little recourse to suppliers if their request is not granted.

DoD staff also asserted that payments get delayed primarily because the supplier made an error in an invoice. This may or may not be true, but a method for resolving such errors in a timely manner seems to be lacking.

Finally, DoD staff described DoD cost-accounting processes as unlikely to pose problems for suppliers because payment is automatic and electronic and because most contracts, being for less than the cost-accounting threshold, do not require a separate certified accounting system. This points to a disconnect between some nontraditional suppliers, who reported problems with cost-accounting processes, and DoD staff, who saw no problem with these processes. This disconnect may reflect problematic processes or a lack of understanding of those processes; either way, it indicates a barrier.

CHAPTER FIVE

Conclusions and Recommendations

The purpose of this study was to answer the question, what barriers do nontraditional suppliers face when trying to work for DoD? The findings from our interviews confirm some barriers to nontraditional suppliers found in earlier research and in Congressional testimony and reveal new ones as well.

Seven of the barriers identified in earlier research and in Congressional testimony were borne out to some degree in our interviews as well. The barriers we heard the most about were:

- the cumbersome, lengthy, and costly bid and selection processes
- the lack of visibility, communication, and information regarding organizations and their requirements.

To a lesser extent, we also heard about

- the unique cost-accounting processes
- restrictions on commercial viability of products, including international sales
- funding uncertainty
- loss of intellectual property or proprietary data
- inadequate advocacy and funding for new technology transition.

We did not hear support for two of the barriers identified in earlier research and in the Congressional hearings during our interviews:

- a perceived DoD preference for large suppliers
- problems with DoD personnel capabilities.

This may have been because we asked about general areas, not about these specific barriers. Finally, we did hear about four other barriers not identified in the earlier research and hearings. These were

- inefficiencies and duplication in the bid process
- incumbent advantage because DoD personnel tend to be risk-averse to new suppliers
- DCMA/DCAA backlogs and turnover that create late payments and inconsistent advice from federal staff
- cumbersome and unhelpful web sites.

These findings point to two areas of recommendations, some that can be implemented immediately and others that address deeper problems and will take longer to implement.

Initial Recommendations

We first note some immediate steps that can be taken without requiring changes to the FAR or Congressional action. These include increasing communication between DoD and suppliers and further streamlining and speeding up the bidding process. Improving communication between DoD and suppliers involves time (and therefore resources) from several kinds of personnel. We recommend that contracting officers be available to answer questions about the bidding process by pointing potential bidders to general information already available on the Small Business Administration web site and answering specific questions about particular RFPs. We also recommend that they provide data on the relative competition in different industries (e.g., the number of firms registered in the CCR by industry and the level of DoD spend by industry) as well as general information on the quality of performance by incumbents. DoD customers (e.g., program officers) could provide more information on their substantive requirements, and engineers could provide more information on technical specifications. All of these ways to increase communication necessarily involve time from personnel who are often already quite busy. DoD leaders, therefore, need to weigh these actions with other priorities for contracting staff and customers.

Further streamlining and speeding the bidding process involves several recommendations as well. First, the parts of the process that vary by service or program could be standardized to reduce the paperwork required, such as requiring copies of bidders' staff resumes and corporate boilerplate repeatedly. Although the DoD process is never going to look like the commercial process, because DoD has different constraints, state and local governments might provide some examples of opportunities for simplification. Second, creating a list of prequalified suppliers would reduce delays and bids with extremely low chances of winning. This could be similar to Government Accountability Office schedules, but without any guarantee of work. Finally, a DoD-wide site could be created in which to put background materials (e.g., employee resumes and company boilerplate) that are otherwise duplicated for each bid. The specific elements from these materials needed for a bid could be identified in the bid, and all of the materials could be updated annually as needed.

Longer-Term Recommendations

Our second tier of recommendations includes those that may be harder to implement because the barriers they address are longstanding. These include, first, further simplify and speed up the final payment processes. This step can reduce the number of supplier-made errors and speeding the final payment from DCAA can be especially helpful for small firms that have less capital.[1] Second, ensure that bidders and DoD staff understand fully the rules around public

---

[1]   As a more general comment on simplifying payments to small businesses, we note that the Obama administration has implemented a Quick Pay Initiative to speed payment to small businesses (Mandelbaum, 2011). But this does not apply to final payments, which DCAA must approve.

release of supplier information. These might include regular reminders of the rules with specific examples that illustrate supplier concerns. Third, reduce the backlogs at DCMA and DCAA, which will likely require more people and more efficient processes. Fourth, assure funding before an RFP is released and when funding cannot be assured, provide the odds of its cancellation. This will require collaboration with the owner of the requirement, as contract staff may not have insight into funding certainty. Finally, removing some enduring barriers may require fundamental changes in how the government does business (e.g., adopting commercial practices). These include using best commercial practices in procurement, payment, supplier relationships, and management of fraud, waste, and abuse. Examples of best commercial practices include combining goods and services into fewer contracts; longer contracts; maximizing automated ordering, invoicing, and payment; developing preferred supplier programs; conducting detailed research on suppliers before contracting; monitoring supplier performance and relationships for irregularities; and requiring that suppliers incorporate these best practices into their own procurement and dealings with suppliers.

Additional Policy Questions

Finally, our findings reveal the need to further explore some policy questions related to contracting. First, how can nontraditional suppliers with no DoD experience better demonstrate their qualifications to contracting officers and customers? Second, how does DoD want contracting officers to balance the priority of expanding the use of nontraditional suppliers, especially small businesses, with the lower risk of using an existing supplier with a strong history of working with DoD? Third, what do contracting officers understand and practice regarding responding to inquiries from bidders? Fourth, is technical evaluation being properly assessed with lowest-price, technically acceptable contracts? Finally, is ITAR being applied as intended? Answers to these policy questions would likely further clarify the reasons behind barriers to nontraditional suppliers to DoD.

Industries Linked to Future DoD Technologies

We reviewed reports assessing future DoD technology requirements to identify industries of future interest to DoD. Only one of the reports specifically linked the technologies to the NAICS of prospective firms, the 2004 Assessment of Industry Attitudes on Collaboration. For the remainder of the reports, we estimated the likely industry based on a description of the technology. Table A.1 summarizes our review and highlights those industries with frequent mention of future technologies/industries as summarized in the right-hand column. Those industries highlighted in green likely had technologies associated with the industry mentioned in eight different reports. Those industries highlighted in yellow had related technologies mentioned in five different reports. Those industries highlighted in tan had related technologies mentioned in four different reports. Those industries highlighted in red had related technologies mentioned in three different reports. Finally, the three industries selected for sampling are indicated in gray. We used this table to select the three industries we sampled for prospective interviewees.

Table A.1
2002 NAICS U.S. Matched to 2007 NAICS U.S.

2002 NAICS Code	2002 NAICS Title[b]	2007 NAICS Code	2007 NAICS Title	2003 (1)	2004 (2)	2010 (3)	2010 (4)	2010 (5)	2011 (6)	2011 (7)	2011 (8)	2011 (9)	Total
313311	Broadwoven Fabric Finishing Mills	313311	Broadwoven Fabric Finishing Mills		x								1
313312	Textile and Fabric Finishing (except Broadwoven Fabric) Mills	313312	Textile and Fabric Finishing (except Broadwoven Fabric) Mills										
313320	Fabric Coating Mills	313320	Fabric Coating Mills		x								1
314911	Textile Bag Mills	314911	Textile Bag Mills		x								1
314912	Canvas and Related Product Mills	314912	Canvas and Related Product Mills		x								1
314991	Rope, Cordage, and Twine Mills	314991	Rope, Cordage, and Twine Mills		x								1
314992	Tire Cord and Tire Fabric Mills	314992	Tire Cord and Tire Fabric Mills		x								1
314999	All Other Miscellaneous Textile Product Mills	314999	All Other Miscellaneous Textile Product Mills		x								1
315211	Men's and Boys' Cut and Sew Apparel Contractors—embroidery contractors	314999	All Other Miscellaneous Textile Product Mills		x								1
315212	Women's, Girls', and Infants' Cut and Sew Apparel Contractors— embroidery contractors	314999	All Other Miscellaneous Textile Product Mills		x								1
322222	Coated and Laminated Paper Manufacturing	322222	Coated and Laminated Paper Manufacturing		x								1
325110	Petrochemical Manufacturing	325110	Petrochemical Manufacturing		x								1
325120	Industrial Gas Manufacturing	325120	Industrial Gas Manufacturing		x								1
325131	Inorganic Dye and Pigment Manufacturing	325131	Inorganic Dye and Pigment Manufacturing		x								1
325132	Synthetic Organic Dye and Pigment Manufacturing	325132	Synthetic Organic Dye and Pigment Manufacturing		x								1

2002 NAICS U.S. Matched to 2007 NAICS U.S. (Full Concordance)[a]

Table A.1 (continued)

| | | | | 2003 | 2004 | 2010 | 2010 | 2010 | 2011 | 2011 | 2011 | 2011 | |
2002 NAICS Code	2002 NAICS Title[b]	2007 NAICS Code	2007 NAICS Title	(1)	(2)	(3)	(4)	(5)	(6)	(7)	(8)	(9)	Total
325181	Alkalies and Chlorine Manufacturing	325181	Alkalies and Chlorine Manufacturing		x								1
325182	Carbon Black Manufacturing	325182	Carbon Black Manufacturing		x								1
325188	All Other Basic Inorganic Chemical Manufacturing	325188	All Other Basic Inorganic Chemical Manufacturing		x								1
325191	Gum and Wood Chemical Manufacturing	325191	Gum and Wood Chemical Manufacturing		x								1
325192	Cyclic Crude and Intermediate Manufacturing	325192	Cyclic Crude and Intermediate Manufacturing		x								1
325193	Ethyl Alcohol Manufacturing	325193	Ethyl Alcohol Manufacturing		x								1
325199	All Other Basic Organic Chemical Manufacturing	325199	All Other Basic Organic Chemical Manufacturing		x								1
325211	Plastics Material and Resin Manufacturing	325211	Plastics Material and Resin Manufacturing		x								1
325212	Synthetic Rubber Manufacturing	325212	Synthetic Rubber Manufacturing		x								1
325221	Cellulosic Organic Fiber Manufacturing	325221	Cellulosic Organic Fiber Manufacturing		x								1
325222	Noncellulosic Organic Fiber Manufacturing	325222	Noncellulosic Organic Fiber Manufacturing		x								1
325510	Paint and Coating Manufacturing	325510	Paint and Coating Manufacturing		x								1
325520	Adhesive Manufacturing	325520	Adhesive Manufacturing		x								1
325611	Soap and Other Detergent Manufacturing	325611	Soap and Other Detergent Manufacturing		x								1

Table A.1 (continued)

2002 NAICS Code	2002 NAICS Title[b]	2007 NAICS Code	2007 NAICS Title[a]	2003 (1)	2004 (2)	2010 (3)	2010 (4)	2010 (5)	2011 (6)	2011 (7)	2011 (8)	2011 (9)	Total
325612	Polish and Other Sanitation Good Manufacturing	325612	Polish and Other Sanitation Good Manufacturing		x								1
325613	Surface Active Agent Manufacturing	325613	Surface Active Agent Manufacturing		x								1
325620	Toilet Preparation Manufacturing	325620	Toilet Preparation Manufacturing		x								1
325910	Printing Ink Manufacturing	325910	Printing Ink Manufacturing		x								1
325920	Explosives Manufacturing	325920	Explosives Manufacturing		x								1
325991	Custom Compounding of Purchased Resins	325991	Custom Compounding of Purchased Resins		x								1
325992	Photographic Film, Paper, Plate, and Chemical Manufacturing	325992	Photographic Film, Paper, Plate, and Chemical Manufacturing		x								1
325998	All Other Miscellaneous Chemical Product and Preparation Manufacturing	325998	All Other Miscellaneous Chemical Product and Preparation Manufacturing		x								1
326111	Plastics Bag Manufacturing	326111	Plastics Bag and Pouch Manufacturing		x								1
326112	Plastics Packaging Film and Sheet (including Laminated) Manufacturing	326112	Plastics Packaging Film and Sheet (including Laminated) Manufacturing		x								1
326113	Unlaminated Plastics Film and Sheet (except Packaging) Manufacturing	326113	Unlaminated Plastics Film and Sheet (except Packaging) Manufacturing		x								1
326121	Unlaminated Plastics Profile Shape Manufacturing	326121	Unlaminated Plastics Profile Shape Manufacturing		x								1

Table A.1 (continued)

2002 NAICS U.S. Matched to 2007 NAICS U.S. (Full Concordance)[a]

2002 NAICS Code	2002 NAICS Title[b]	2007 NAICS Code	2007 NAICS Title	2003 (1)	2004 (2)	2010 (3)	2010 (4)	2010 (5)	2011 (6)	2011 (7)	2011 (8)	2011 (9)	Total
326122	Plastics Pipe and Pipe Fitting Manufacturing	326122	Plastics Pipe and Pipe Fitting Manufacturing		x								1
326130	Laminated Plastics Plate, Sheet (except Packaging), and Shape Manufacturing	326130	Laminated Plastics Plate, Sheet (except Packaging), and Shape Manufacturing		x								1
326140	Polystyrene Foam Product Manufacturing	326140	Polystyrene Foam Product Manufacturing		x								1
326150	Urethane and Other Foam Product (except Polystyrene) Manufacturing	326150	Urethane and Other Foam Product (except Polystyrene) Manufacturing		x								1
326160	Plastics Bottle Manufacturing	326160	Plastics Bottle Manufacturing		x								1
326191	Plastics Plumbing Fixture Manufacturing	326191	Plastics Plumbing Fixture Manufacturing		x								1
326192	Resilient Floor Covering Manufacturing	326192	Resilient Floor Covering Manufacturing		x								1
326199	All Other Plastics Product Manufacturing—except inflatable plastic boats	326199	All Other Plastics Product Manufacturing		x								1
327212	Other Pressed and Blown Glass and Glassware Manufacturing	327212	Other Pressed and Blown Glass and Glassware Manufacturing		x								1
331491	Nonferrous Metal (except Copper and Aluminum) Rolling, Drawing, and Extruding	331491	Nonferrous Metal (except Copper and Aluminum) Rolling, Drawing, and Extruding		x								1
331492	Secondary Smelting, Refining, and Alloying of Nonferrous Metal (except Copper and Aluminum)	331492	Secondary Smelting, Refining, and Alloying of Nonferrous Metal (except Copper and Aluminum)		x								1

Table A.1 (continued)

	2002 NAICS U.S. Matched to 2007 NAICS U.S. (Full Concordance)[a]											
2002 NAICS Code	2002 NAICS Title[b]	2007 NAICS Code	2007 NAICS Title	2003 (1)	2004 (2)	2010 (3)	2010 (4)	2010 (5)	2011 (6)	2011 (7)	2011 (8)	2011 (9)	Total
331512	Steel Investment Foundries	331512	Steel Investment Foundries		x								1
332311	Prefabricated Metal Building and Component Manufacturing	332311	Prefabricated Metal Building and Component Manufacturing		x								1
332312	Fabricated Structural Metal Manufacturing	332312	Fabricated Structural Metal Manufacturing		x								1
332313	Plate Work Manufacturing	332313	Plate Work Manufacturing		x								1
332321	Metal Window and Door Manufacturing	332321	Metal Window and Door Manufacturing		x								1
332322	Sheet Metal Work Manufacturing	332322	Sheet Metal Work Manufacturing		x								1
332323	Ornamental and Architectural Metal Work Manufacturing	332323	Ornamental and Architectural Metal Work Manufacturing		x								1
332811	Metal Heat Treating	332811	Metal Heat Treating		x								1
332812	Metal Coating, Engraving (except Jewelry and Silverware), and Allied Services to Manufacturers	332812	Metal Coating, Engraving (except Jewelry and Silverware), and Allied Services to Manufacturers		x								1
332813	Electroplating, Plating, Polishing, Anodizing, and Coloring	332813	Electroplating, Plating, Polishing, Anodizing, and Coloring		x								1
332911	Industrial Valve Manufacturing	332911	Industrial Valve Manufacturing		x								1
332912	Fluid Power Valve and Hose Fitting Manufacturing	332912	Fluid Power Valve and Hose Fitting Manufacturing		x								1
332913	Plumbing Fixture Fitting and Trim Manufacturing	332913	Plumbing Fixture Fitting and Trim Manufacturing		x								1

Table A.1 (continued)

2002 NAICS U.S. Matched to 2007 NAICS U.S. (Full Concordance)[a]

2002 NAICS Code	2002 NAICS Title[b]	2007 NAICS Code	2007 NAICS Title	2003 (1)	2004 (2)	2010 (3)	2010 (4)	2010 (5)	2011 (6)	2011 (7)	2011 (8)	2011 (9)	Total
332919	Other Metal Valve and Pipe Fitting Manufacturing	332919	Other Metal Valve and Pipe Fitting Manufacturing		x								1
332991	Ball and Roller Bearing Fitting Manufacturing	332991	Ball and Roller Bearing Fitting Manufacturing		x								1
332992	Small Arms Ammunition Manufacturing	332992	Small Arms Ammunition Manufacturing		x								1
332993	Ammunition (except Small Arms) Manufacturing	332993	Ammunition (except Small Arms) Manufacturing		x								1
332994	Small Arms Manufacturing	332994	Small Arms Manufacturing		x							x	2
332995	Other Ordnance and Accessories Manufacturing	332995	Other Ordnance and Accessories Manufacturing		x								1
332996	Fabricated Pipe and Pipe Fitting Manufacturing	332996	Fabricated Pipe and Pipe Fitting Manufacturing		x								1
332997	Industrial Pattern Manufacturing	332997	Industrial Pattern Manufacturing		x								1
332998	Enameled Iron and Metal Sanitary Ware Manufacturing	332998	Enameled Iron and Metal Sanitary Ware Manufacturing		x								1
332999	All Other Miscellaneous Fabricated Metal Product Manufacturing	332999	All Other Miscellaneous Fabricated Metal Product Manufacturing		x								1
333291	Paper Industry Machinery Manufacturing	333291	Paper Industry Machinery Manufacturing		x								1
333292	Textile Machinery Manufacturing	333292	Textile Machinery Manufacturing		x								1
333293	Printing Machinery and Equipment Manufacturing	333293	Printing Machinery and Equipment Manufacturing		x								1

Table A.1 (continued)

2002 NAICS U.S. Matched to 2007 NAICS U.S. (Full Concordance)[a]

2002 NAICS Code	2002 NAICS Title[b]	2007 NAICS Code	2007 NAICS Title	2003 (1)	2004 (2)	2010 (3)	2010 (4)	2010 (5)	2011 (6)	2011 (7)	2011 (8)	2011 (9)	Total
333294	Food Product Machinery Manufacturing	333294	Food Product Machinery Manufacturing		x								1
333295	Semiconductor Machinery Manufacturing	333295	Semiconductor Machinery Manufacturing		x								1
333298	All Other Industrial Machinery Manufacturing	333298	All Other Industrial Machinery Manufacturing		x								1
333314	Optical Instrument and Lens Manufacturing	333314	Optical Instrument and Lens Manufacturing							x			1
333319	Other Commercial and Service Industry Machinery Manufacturing	333319	Other Commercial and Service Industry Machinery Manufacturing	x								x	2
333415	Air-Conditioning and Warm Air Heating Equipment and Commercial and Industrial Refrigeration Equipment Manufacturing	333415	Air-Conditioning and Warm Air Heating Equipment and Commercial and Industrial Refrigeration Equipment Manufacturing					x					1
333611	Turbine and Turbine Generator Set Units Manufacturing	333611	Turbine and Turbine Generator Set Units Manufacturing		x			x					2
333992	Welding and Soldering Equipment Manufacturing	333992	Welding and Soldering Equipment Manufacturing		x								1
333999	All Other Miscellaneous General Purpose Machinery Manufacturing	333999	All Other Miscellaneous General Purpose Machinery Manufacturing		x								1
334111	Electronic Computer Manufacturing	334111	Electronic Computer Manufacturing		x	x						x	3
334112	Computer Storage Device Manufacturing	334112	Computer Storage Device Manufacturing		x								1

Table A.1 (continued)

2002 NAICS U.S. Matched to 2007 NAICS U.S. (Full Concordance)[a]

2002 NAICS Code	2002 NAICS Title[b]	2007 NAICS Code	2007 NAICS Title	2003 (1)	2004 (2)	2010 (3)	2010 (4)	2010 (5)	2011 (6)	2011 (7)	2011 (8)	2011 (9)	Total
334113	Computer Terminal Manufacturing	334113	Computer Terminal Manufacturing		x								1
334119	Other Computer Peripheral Equipment Manufacturing	334119	Other Computer Peripheral Equipment Manufacturing		x								1
334210	Telephone Apparatus Manufacturing	334210	Telephone Apparatus Manufacturing		x								1
334220	Radio and Television Broadcasting and Wireless Communications Equipment Manufacturing—except communications signal testing and evaluation equipment	334220	Radio and Television Broadcasting and Wireless Communications Equipment Manufacturing		x	x				x			3
334290	Other Communications Equipment Manufacturing	334290	Other Communications Equipment Manufacturing		x								1
334310	Audio and Video Equipment Manufacturing	334310	Audio and Video Equipment Manufacturing		x								1
334411	Electron Tube Manufacturing	334411	Electron Tube Manufacturing		x								1
334412	Bare Printed Circuit Board Manufacturing	334412	Bare Printed Circuit Board Manufacturing		x								1
334413	Semiconductor and Related Device Manufacturing	334413	Semiconductor and Related Device Manufacturing		x				x			x	3
334414	Electronic Capacitor Manufacturing	334414	Electronic Capacitor Manufacturing		x								1
334415	Electronic Resistor Manufacturing	334415	Electronic Resistor Manufacturing		x								1
334416	Electronic Coil, Transformer, and Other Inductor Manufacturing	334416	Electronic Coil, Transformer, and Other Inductor Manufacturing		x								1

Table A.1 (continued)

2002 NAICS U.S. Matched to 2007 NAICS U.S. (Full Concordance)[a]

2002 NAICS Code	2002 NAICS Title[b]	2007 NAICS Code	2007 NAICS Title	2003 (1)	2004 (2)	2010 (3)	2010 (4)	2010 (5)	2011 (6)	2011 (7)	2011 (8)	2011 (9)	Total
334417	Electronic Connector Manufacturing	334417	Electronic Connector Manufacturing		x								1
334418	Printed Circuit Assembly (Electronic Assembly) Manufacturing	334418	Printed Circuit Assembly (Electronic Assembly) Manufacturing		x								1
334419	Other Electronic Component Manufacturing	334419	Other Electronic Component Manufacturing		x								1
334510	Electromedical and Electrotherapeutic Apparatus Manufacturing	334510	Electromedical and Electrotherapeutic Apparatus Manufacturing		x								1
334511	Search, Detection, Navigation, Guidance, Aeronautical, and Nautical System and Instrument Manufacturing	334511	Search, Detection, Navigation, Guidance, Aeronautical, and Nautical System and Instrument Manufacturing	x	x	x	x	x		x	x	x	8
334512	Automatic Environmental Control Manufacturing for Residential, Commercial, and Appliance Use	334512	Automatic Environmental Control Manufacturing for Residential, Commercial, and Appliance Use		x								1
334513	Instruments and Related Products Manufacturing for Measuring, Displaying, and Controlling Industrial Process Variables	334513	Instruments and Related Products Manufacturing for Measuring, Displaying, and Controlling Industrial Process Variables		x								1
334514	Totalizing Fluid Meter and Counting Device Manufacturing	334514	Totalizing Fluid Meter and Counting Device Manufacturing		x								1
334515	Instrument Manufacturing for Measuring and Testing Electricity and Electrical Signals	334515	Instrument Manufacturing for Measuring and Testing Electricity and Electrical Signals		x								1

Table A.1 (continued)

2002 NAICS U.S. Matched to 2007 NAICS U.S. (Full Concordance)[a]

2002 NAICS Code	2002 NAICS Title[b]	2007 NAICS Code	2007 NAICS Title	2003 (1)	2004 (2)	2010 (3)	2010 (4)	2010 (5)	2011 (6)	2011 (7)	2011 (8)	2011 (9)	Total
334516	Analytical Laboratory Instrument Manufacturing	334516	Analytical Laboratory Instrument Manufacturing		x								1
334517	Irradiation Apparatus Manufacturing	334517	Irradiation Apparatus Manufacturing		x								1
334518	Watch, Clock, and Part Manufacturing	334518	Watch, Clock, and Part Manufacturing		x								1
334519	Other Measuring and Controlling Device Manufacturing	334519	Other Measuring and Controlling Device Manufacturing		x								1
335311	Power, Distribution, and Specialty Transformer Manufacturing	335311	Power, Distribution, and Specialty Transformer Manufacturing		x								1
335312	Motor and Generator Manufacturing	335312	Motor and Generator Manufacturing		x								1
335313	Switchgear and Switchboard Apparatus Manufacturing	335313	Switchgear and Switchboard Apparatus Manufacturing		x								1
335314	Relay and Industrial Control Manufacturing	335314	Relay and Industrial Control Manufacturing		x								1
335911	Storage Battery Manufacturing	335911	Storage Battery Manufacturing		x								1
335912	Primary Battery Manufacturing	335912	Primary Battery Manufacturing		x								1
335921	Fiber Optic Cable Manufacturing	335921	Fiber Optic Cable Manufacturing		x								1
335929	Other Communication and Energy Wire Manufacturing	335929	Other Communication and Energy Wire Manufacturing		x								1

Table A.1 (continued)

2002 NAICS Code	2002 NAICS Title[b]	2007 NAICS Code	2007 NAICS Title	2003 (1)	2004 (2)	2010 (3)	2010 (4)	2010 (5)	2011 (6)	2011 (7)	2011 (8)	2011 (9)	Total
335931	Current-Carrying Wiring Device Manufacturing	335931	Current-Carrying Wiring Device Manufacturing		x								1
335932	Noncurrent-Carrying Wiring Device Manufacturing	335932	Noncurrent-Carrying Wiring Device Manufacturing		x								1
335991	Carbon and Graphite Product Manufacturing	335991	Carbon and Graphite Product Manufacturing	x	x								2
335999	All Other Miscellaneous Electrical Equipment and Component Manufacturing	335999	All Other Miscellaneous Electrical Equipment and Component Manufacturing		x							x	2
336111	Automobile Manufacturing	336111	Automobile Manufacturing		x		x	x					3
336112	Light Truck and Utility Vehicle Manufacturing	336112	Light Truck and Utility Vehicle Manufacturing					x					1
336311	Carburetor, Piston, Piston Ring, and Valve Manufacturing	336311	Carburetor, Piston, Piston Ring, and Valve Manufacturing		x								1
336312	Gasoline Engine and Engine Parts Manufacturing	336312	Gasoline Engine and Engine Parts Manufacturing		x								1
336321	Vehicular Lighting Equipment Manufacturing	336321	Vehicular Lighting Equipment Manufacturing		x								1
336322	Other Motor Vehicle Electrical and Electronic Equipment Manufacturing	336322	Other Motor Vehicle Electrical and Electronic Equipment Manufacturing		x			x					2
336330	Motor Vehicle Steering and Suspension Components (except Spring) Manufacturing	336330	Motor Vehicle Steering and Suspension Components (except Spring) Manufacturing		x								1

2002 NAICS U.S. Matched to 2007 NAICS U.S. (Full Concordance)[a]

Table A.1 (continued)

2002 NAICS Code	2002 NAICS Title[b]	2007 NAICS Code	2007 NAICS Title	2003 (1)	2004 (2)	2010 (3)	2010 (4)	2010 (5)	2011 (6)	2011 (7)	2011 (8)	2011 (9)	Total
336340	Motor Vehicle Brake System Manufacturing	336340	Motor Vehicle Brake System Manufacturing		x								1
336350	Motor Vehicle Transmission and Power Train Parts Manufacturing	336350	Motor Vehicle Transmission and Power Train Parts Manufacturing		x								1
336360	Motor Vehicle Seating and Interior Trim Manufacturing	336360	Motor Vehicle Seating and Interior Trim Manufacturing		x								1
336370	Motor Vehicle Metal Stamping	336370	Motor Vehicle Metal Stamping		x								1
336391	Motor Vehicle Air-Conditioning Manufacturing	336391	Motor Vehicle Air-Conditioning Manufacturing		x								1
336399	All Other Motor Vehicle Parts Manufacturing	336399	All Other Motor Vehicle Parts Manufacturing		x								1
336411	Aircraft Manufacturing	336411	Aircraft Manufacturing	x	x		x	x					4
336412	Aircraft Engine and Engine Parts Manufacturing	336412	Aircraft Engine and Engine Parts Manufacturing		x								1
336413	Other Aircraft Parts and Auxiliary Equipment Manufacturing	336413	Other Aircraft Parts and Auxiliary Equipment Manufacturing		x								1
336414	Guided Missile and Space Vehicle Manufacturing	336414	Guided Missile and Space Vehicle Manufacturing		x		x						2
336415	Guided Missile and Space Vehicle Propulsion Unit and Propulsion Unit Parts Manufacturing	336415	Guided Missile and Space Vehicle Propulsion Unit and Propulsion Unit Parts Manufacturing		x			x					2

Table A.1 (continued)

2002 NAICS U.S. Matched to 2007 NAICS U.S. (Full Concordance)[a]				2003	2004	2010	2010	2010	2011	2011	2011	2011	Total
2002 NAICS Code	2002 NAICS Title[b]	2007 NAICS Code	2007 NAICS Title	(1)	(2)	(3)	(4)	(5)	(6)	(7)	(8)	(9)	
336419	Other Guided Missile and Space Vehicle Parts and Auxiliary Equipment Manufacturing	336419	Other Guided Missile and Space Vehicle Parts and Auxiliary Equipment Manufacturing		x								1
336611	Ship Building and Repairing	336611	Ship Building and Repairing		x								1
336992	Military Armored Vehicle, Tank, and Tank Component Manufacturing	336992	Military Armored Vehicle, Tank, and Tank Component Manufacturing		x		x						2
339111	Laboratory Apparatus and Furniture Manufacturing—except laboratory distilling equipment, freezers, furnaces, ovens, scales, balances, centrifuges, and furniture	339113	Surgical Appliance and Supplies Manufacturing		x								1
339113	Surgical Appliance and Supplies Manufacturing	339113	Surgical Appliance and Supplies Manufacturing		x							x	2
339911	Jewelry (except Costume) Manufacturing	339911	Jewelry (except Costume) Manufacturing		x								1
339912	Silverware and Hollowware Manufacturing	339912	Silverware and Hollowware Manufacturing		x								1
339913	Jewelers' Material and Lapidary Work Manufacturing	339913	Jewelers' Material and Lapidary Work Manufacturing		x								1
339914	Costume Jewelry and Novelty Manufacturing	339914	Costume Jewelry and Novelty Manufacturing		x								1
339920	Sporting and Athletic Goods Manufacturing	339920	Sporting and Athletic Goods Manufacturing		x								1
339931	Doll and Stuffed Toy Manufacturing	339931	Doll and Stuffed Toy Manufacturing		x								1

Table A.1 (continued)

2002 NAICS Code	2002 NAICS Title[b]	2007 NAICS Code	2007 NAICS Title	2003 (1)	2004 (2)	2010 (3)	2010 (4)	2010 (5)	2011 (6)	2011 (7)	2011 (8)	2011 (9)	Total
	2002 NAICS U.S. Matched to 2007 NAICS U.S. (Full Concordance)[a]												
339932	Game, Toy, and Children's Vehicle Manufacturing	339932	Game, Toy, and Children's Vehicle Manufacturing		x								1
339941	Pen and Mechanical Pencil Manufacturing	339941	Pen and Mechanical Pencil Manufacturing		x								1
339942	Lead Pencil and Art Good Manufacturing	339942	Lead Pencil and Art Good Manufacturing		x								1
339943	Marking Device Manufacturing	339943	Marking Device Manufacturing		x								1
339944	Carbon Paper and Inked Ribbon Manufacturing	339944	Carbon Paper and Inked Ribbon Manufacturing		x								1
339950	Sign Manufacturing	339950	Sign Manufacturing		x								1
339991	Gasket, Packing, and Sealing Device Manufacturing	339991	Gasket, Packing, and Sealing Device Manufacturing		x								1
339992	Musical Instrument Manufacturing	339992	Musical Instrument Manufacturing		x								1
339993	Fastener, Button, Needle, and Pin Manufacturing	339993	Fastener, Button, Needle, and Pin Manufacturing		x								1
339994	Broom, Brush, and Mop Manufacturing	339994	Broom, Brush, and Mop Manufacturing		x								1
339995	Burial Casket Manufacturing	339995	Burial Casket Manufacturing		x								1
339999	All Other Miscellaneous Manufacturing	339999	All Other Miscellaneous Manufacturing		x								1
424210	Drugs and Druggists' Sundries Merchant Wholesalers	424210	Drugs and Druggists' Sundries Merchant Wholesalers	x									1
441310	Automotive Parts and Accessories Stores	441310	Automotive Parts and Accessories Stores		x								1

Table A.1 (continued)

2002 NAICS Code	2002 NAICS Title[b]	2007 NAICS Code	2007 NAICS Title	2003 (1)	2004 (2)	2010 (3)	2010 (4)	2010 (5)	2011 (6)	2011 (7)	2011 (8)	2011 (9)	Total
441320	Tire Dealers	441320	Tire Dealers		x								1
511210	Software Publishers	511210	Software Publishers		x								1
517910	Other Telecommunications	517919	All Other Telecommunications		x								1
518111	Internet Service Providers—Internet services providers providing services via client-supplied telecommunications connection	517919	All Other Telecommunications		x								1
541330	Engineering Services	541330	Engineering Services		x		x						2
541511	Custom Computer Programming Services	541511	Custom Computer Programming Services		x	x	x			x		x	5
541512	Computer Systems Design Services	541512	Computer Systems Design Services	x	x	x	x						4
541710	Research and Development in the Physical, Engineering, and Life Sciences—biotechnology research and development	541711	Research and Development in Biotechnology		x		x		x				3
541710	Research and Development in the Physical, Engineering, and Life Sciences—except biotechnology research and development	541712	Research and Development in the Physical, Engineering, and Life Sciences (except Biotechnology)		x	x	x	x				x	5
541720	Research and Development in the Social Sciences and Humanities	541720	Research and Development in the Social Sciences and Humanities		x	x							2
541910	Marketing Research and Public Opinion Polling	541910	Marketing Research and Public Opinion Polling		x								1
561990	All Other Support Services	561990	All Other Support Services		x								1

NOTES: Full information for the table column heads is as follows: (1) Transforming the Defense Industrial Base: A Roadmap; (2) Assessment of Industry Attitudes on Collaboration with DoD; (3) Report on Technology Horizons: A Vision for Air Force Science and Technology; (4) Survivability/Lethality Analysis—Army; (5) Vehicle Technology Directorate; (6) DoD Mico Electronics Study; (7) DoD TechMatch.com; (8) Defence Venture Catalyst Initiative; and (9) Techology Areas of Interest ARL.
[a]Wording for NAICS column headings were taken directly from the U.S. Census (U.S. Department of Commerce, undated). 2007 NAICS codes in bold indicate that pieces of the 2007 industry came from more than one 2002 NAICS industry; 2002 NAICS codes in italics indicate that the 2002 industry split to two or more 2007 industries.
[b](and specific piece of the 2002 industry that is contained in the 2007 industry).

Interview Protocols: Business Interview Protocol for RAND Study

Identification of Barriers to Non-Traditional DoD Suppliers with Recommendations for Elimination

Sponsored by Office of Small Business Programs, Office of the Under Secretary of Defense, Department of Defense

We have been asked by the Office of Small Business Programs to analyze potential barriers to non-traditional companies seeking to do business with the Department of Defense (DoD). Nontraditional companies are those that have less than $500,000 of business with the DoD. The purpose of this interview is to identify barriers to the application and procurement processes of the DoD. We will not reveal the names of persons or companies we interview. Rather, we plan to aggregate our findings across all of our interviews and characterize our findings in a general way. Your participation in this study is voluntary, and you may choose not to answer any or all of the questions that follow.

Background Questions:

1. Please describe your history with Department of Defense and other federal government contracts.
    a.   How many contracts and for what length of time
    b.   Whether you applied for contracts that you did not receive
    c.   Prime contracts of your own and subcontracts on another firm's contract

2. Is your business considered a small business according to the Small Business Administration thresholds?

3. Does your business qualify for any commercial sector or government socioeconomic goals? [prompt: women-owned, veteran-owned, service disabled veteran-owned, Native American owned, located in a HUBZone]

Potential Barriers:

4. Do you believe or have you experienced that winning contracts with the Department of Defense is easier or harder than in the commercial sector? Please explain.

[Prompt with:] Is this because:
a.   Competition is greater or lesser? Please explain.
b.   Small business goals for particular types of small or disadvantaged businesses? Please explain.

5.   Contracting with the Department of Defense can involve time and money that contracting with commercial companies doesn't require. Have you spent time or money on
a Department of Defense contract that you don't spend on a commercial contract? If
yes, please describe the things you had to do for a DoD contract that you do not typically have to do for a commercial contract.

[Prompts]
a.   Getting a security clearance
b.   Acquisition procedures or regulations that take your regular employees away from
their other work
c.   Acquisition procedures or regulations that require additional employees to
process
d.   Acquisition procedures or regulations that require specialized employees to
process
e.   Acquisition processes that take a long time to award contracts
f.   Recent increases in interim acquisition rules
g.   Procurement procedures that require technology before procurement process
begins
h.   Disclosure requirements
i.   Increases in requirements for disclosure because of an adversarial relationship
between the government office and suppliers
j.   Payment procedures that take a long time to pay contractors.
   i.   Has the Quick Pay Initiative from September 2011 affected this?

6.   Please estimate the additional time and cost involved with these extra tasks when apply-
ing for a contract.

7.   Have any of these things made you less likely to apply for a Department of Defense
contract?

8.   Contracting with the Department of Defense can involve risks for your company that
contracting with commercial companies doesn't involve. Are there any risks you have
experienced with a DoD contract? If yes, please describe.

[Prompts]
a.   Risk of wasting time and money in a proposal because an RFP gets pulled after
it was published (but before award)
b.   Risk of firm's vulnerable areas being made public because of disclosure
requirements
c.   Risk of losing intellectual property because required technical specs became
available to the competition before a proposal was awarded

    d.   Risk of losing intellectual property rights for other reasons

    e.   Risky joint ventures with other companies because your company cannot do all the work required in the solicitation

9.   Have any of these risks made you less likely to apply for a Department of Defense contract? If so, which ones deter you the most?

10.   [Small business owners only] Contracting with the Department of Defense can differ for small business owners and for larger business owners. Are there things that make contracting with the Department of Defense difficult for you as a small business owner? If yes, please describe.

    [Prompts]
    a.   Small business size thresholds at a level that poses problems
    b.   IDIQs [Indefinite Delivery, Indefinite Quantity] that make the contract too large for a small firm
    c.   Bundled contract that makes the contract too large for a small firm
    d.   Other contracts that are too large for a small firm
    e.   Lack of the internal research and development money that large business have to invest in proposals
    f.   Lack of resources to keep employees on salary while waiting for a contract award because of long lead times prior to selection and timing of contract payments
    g.   Lack of money for test and evaluation to get a new innovation ready for military procurement
    h.   Need for resources to make your firm viable to bid (e.g., capital improvements, insurance bonds)
    i.   Lack of available market research on small and nontraditional firms that PMs [Program Managers] could use to ensure that a small business is qualified and viable
    j.   Emphasis on "lowest price, technically acceptable" because small firms cannot afford the lowest bidding price
    k.   Less access to DoD to communicate businesses' needs and capabilities

11.   Have any of these small business issues made you less likely to apply for a Department of Defense contract?

12.   Are there other federal rules or practices that make the contracting process with the Department of Defense difficult? If yes, please describe.

    [Prompts]
    a.   Lack of communication between Department of Defense and industry about DoD needs and businesses' capabilities
    b.   Lack of understanding or clarity about DoD contracting procedures
    c.   Emphasis on "lowest price, technically acceptable" that discourages innovation and encourages counterfeits

    d.   Long time between development of an innovation and getting the money for it appropriated into the federal budget to pay for full procurement

    e.   Definition of "inherently governmental" too broad

    f.   Inadequate funding for the contract

    g.   Negative perception by private investors

    h.   Longer product cycles

    i.   Federal contract staff who do not answer questions sufficiently

    j.   Federal contract staff who go with a known and proven firm rather than conduct the analysis necessary to work with a nontraditional supplier

    k.   The International Traffic in Arms Regulation of 2011 (ITAR)

    l.   Federal contracting culture and requirements that focus on avoiding mistakes rather than on finding innovation or best quality

13. Have any of these other issues made you less likely to apply for a Department of Defense contract?

14. Are there other things that make contracting with the Department of Defense difficult? If yes, please describe.

15. If the DoD could change one thing that would make its business more attractive to you, what would that be?

DoD Staff Interview Protocol for RAND Study

Identification of Barriers to Non-Traditional DoD Suppliers with Recommendations for Elimination Sponsored by Office of Small Business Programs, Office of the Under Secretary of Defense, Department of Defense

The Department of Defense (DoD) has been asked by Congress to analyze potential barriers to nontraditional companies seeking to do business with the DoD. Nontraditional companies are those that have less than $500,000 of business with the DoD. The DoD's Office of Small Business Programs, in turn, has asked RAND to undertake the analysis. This interview is part of that study, and its purpose is to understand the process of doing business with nontraditional suppliers and to learn about possible barriers that they may face. We will not reveal the names of persons or offices we interview. Rather, we plan to aggregate our findings across all of our interviews and characterize our findings in a general way. Your participation in this study is voluntary, and you may choose not to answer any or all of the questions that follow.

    Throughout these questions, please refer to whichever branches of the armed forces apply to your experience.

Background Questions

1. Please describe your position.

2. Do you work with nontraditional suppliers?

3. How long have you worked in this position?

Learning About Opportunities

4. What are the mechanisms/channels available for potential suppliers to learn more about bidding opportunities? Do you know of any plans to improve the search or interface capabilities of the web sites involved?

5. Once a company identifies an opportunity and has questions about their fit for what's required, how do they determine whom to call to learn more about those requirements?

6. Some companies could not get their inquiries returned. How can companies get answers to questions about requirements?

7. For specific solicitations, are there any practices for reaching out to nontraditional suppliers and encouraging them to apply? Is there anyone else we should talk to about practices like these?

8. When a company bids on a contract and does not win, is there a way for the company to receive feedback on how to improve their future bids? Please describe.

Bidding Process

9. In your experience, does the process of bidding for a DoD contract encourage or discourage new bidders? Please explain. Has this process gotten easier or harder over time?

10. Are you aware of any plans or programs for streamlining the process?

11. If a supplier has a question about the bidding process, how do they determine whom to call to answer that question?

12. Some companies could not get their inquiries returned. How can companies get answers to questions about the bidding process?

Contract Management

13. Once a company wins a contract, how do they work with DoD to manage it smoothly?

14. Who do they work with? Does this same person or office remain for the length of the contract?

15. If there is a problem after the contract is signed, how can it get resolved?

Funding Time Line

16.   Some suppliers described difficulties that can arise, especially for small businesses, from delays or gaps in funding or payments. Is this an issue that small business advocates are aware of? Are there any plans for speeding up the funding or payment time lines or for eliminating delays? Please describe.

Accounting Practices

17.   In your experience, do DoD's accounting practices encourage or discourage new suppliers from bidding on more contracts? Please explain.

18.   If suppliers have trouble with DoD accounting, how do they resolve the problem?

Small Business Programs

19.   In your experience, do small business set-aside programs encourage firms that qualify for these programs to become new DoD suppliers? Please explain.

20.   In your experience, do small business set-aside programs encourage firms that do not qualify for these programs to become new DoD suppliers? Please explain.

International Sales Limitations

21.   In your experience, have ITAR requirements discouraged nontraditional suppliers from bidding on DoD contracts?

22.   Are you aware of any plans or practices to apply ITAR more selectively?

Prior Successful DoD Experience

23.   Some suppliers believe their chances of winning a bid are extremely low because they have no prior DoD contracting experience or no experience with a specific office. In your experience, what's the best way for new suppliers to break into the game?

Conclusion

24.   In your experience, what barriers have you observed that nontraditional suppliers face in trying to win DoD contracts?

Bibliography

Air Force Office of Scientific Research, "Dynamical Systems and Control (RTA)," November 23, 2011, As of March 28, 2013:
http://www.wpafb.af.mil/library/factsheets/factsheet.asp?id=9196

Air Force Office of Scientific Research, "Information, Decision and Complex Networks (RTC)," October 24, 2011. As of March 28, 2013:
http://www.wpafb.af.mil/library/factsheets/factsheet.asp?id=9204

Air Force Office of Scientific Research, "Quantum and Non-Equilibrium Processes (RTB)," September 23, 2011. As of March 28, 2013:
http://www.wpafb.af.mil/library/factsheets/factsheet.asp?id=9205

Air Force Office of Scientific Research, "Broad Agency Announcements," Current. As of February 20, 2012:
http://www.wpafb.af.mil/library/factsheets/factsheet.asp?id=8127

Andrews, Robert E., "Testimony Before the House Armed Services Subcommittee on Defense Acquisition Reform," October 29, 2009.

"Armed Services Committee Panel Meets with California Businesses," *Congressional Documents and Publications,* January 9, 2012.

"Armed Services Committee Panel Meets with Hawaii Businesses," *Congressional Documents and Publications,* January 10, 2012.

Army Research Laboratory, Technology Areas of Interest, March 16, 2011. As of February 20, 2012:
http://www.arl.army.mil/

Army Research Laboratory, Vehicle Technology Directorate, "Intelligent Systems, Propulsion, Platform, Logistics," March 11, 2011. As of February 20, 2012:
http://www.arl.army.mil/www/default.cfm?page=34

Army Research Laboratory, ARL Technology, Survivability/Lethality Analysis, "Ballistic Vulnerability/ Lethality (V/L), Electronic Warfare, Information Assurance/Computer Network Defense (IA/CND), System of Systems (SoS)," September 1, 2010. As of February 20, 2012:
http://www.arl.army.mil/www/default.cfm?page=147

Army Research Laboratory, "Simulation and Training Technology," December 8, 2010. As of February 20, 2012:
http://www.arl.army.mil/www/default.cfm?page=540

Avent, Randy K., "OSD Data-to-Decisions Strategic Initiatives," February 28, 2011, As of March 28, 2013:
http://www.onr.navy.mil/~/media/Files/Funding-Announcements/Special-Notice/ 2011/11-SN-0004-Amendment-0002-1.ashx

Barr, Steven H., Ted Baker, Steven K. Markham, and Angus J. Kingon, "Bridging the Valley of Death: Lessons Learned from 14 Years of Commercialization of Technology Education," *Journal of the Academy of Management Learning and Education,* Vol. 8, No. 3, September 2009.

"Business Panel Meets to Discuss Challenges within the Defense Industry," *Targeted News Service,* February 21, 2012.

Butler, Amy, "Pentagon Opens Door to Lower-Tier Industrial Consolidation," *Aviation Week and Space Technology,* February 14, 2011.

"Congressmen Conaway and Andrews Applaud New HASC Business Panel," *States News Service,* September 21, 2011.

"Cyclone Power Technologies Participates in House Armed Services Roundtable to Assist Small Businesses," *Business Wire,* February 22, 2012.

Department of Commerce, Bureau of Industry and Security, "Assessment of Industry Attitudes on Collaborating with the U.S. Department of Defense in Research and Development and Technology Sharing," January 2004. As of July 21, 2011:
http://www.bis.doc.gov/defenseindustrialbaseprograms/osies/defmarketresearchrpts/research_and_development_study.pdf

Department of Homeland Security, "A Roadmap for Cybersecurity Research," November 2009. As of February 20, 2012:
http://www.cyber.st.dhs.gov/docs/DHS-Cybersecurity-Roadmap.pdf

DoDTechMatch.com, "Browse Hot Technologies," As of February 20, 2012:
http://www.dodtechmatch.com/DOD/TECHAD/BROWSE.ASPX?TYPE=BROWSE

Erwin, Sandra I., "For High-Tech Firms, Allure of Defense Contracts is Tarnished by Red Tape," *National Defense,* February 2011. As of July 21, 2011:
http://www.nationaldefensemagazine.org/archive/2011/February/Pages/
ForHigh-TechFirms,AllureofDefenseContractsIsTarnishedbyRedTape.aspx

Federal Procurement Data System, "Top 100 Contractors Report for Fiscal Year 2010," 2011. As of July 20, 2011:
https://www.fpds.gov/downloads/top_requests/Top_100_Contractors_Report_Fiscal_Year_2010.xls

"First Hearing Set for Tuesday; New House Panel Aims to Propose Legislation, Level Defense Field," *Inside the Pentagon,* September 15, 2011.

Gansler, Jacques S., *Democracy's Arsenal: Creating a Twenty-First Century Defense Industry,* Cambridge, Mass.: The MIT Press, 2011.

"Georgia Tech's EVP for Research Testifies before House Armed Services Committee," *Targeted News Service,* January 23, 2012.

Government Accountability Office, "Further Action Needed to Promote Successful Use of Special DHS Acquisition Authority," December 2004. As of July 21, 2011:
http://www.gao.gov/new.items/d05136.pdf

Government Accountability Office, "Managing the Supplier Base in the 21st Century," March 2006. As of July 21, 2011:
http://www.gao.gov/new.items/d06533sp.pdf

Government Accountability Office, "Improvements Could Further Enhance Ability to Acquire Innovative Technologies Using Other Transaction Authority," September 2008. As of July 21, 2011:
http://www.gao.gov/new.items/d081088.pdf

Grasso, Valerie Bailey, "Defense Acquisition Reform: Status and Current Issues," Washington, D.C.: Congressional Research Service, May 16, 2003.

Grasso, Valerie Bailey, "Defense Logistical Support Contracts in Iraq and Afghanistan: Issues for Congress," Washington, D.C., Congressional Research Service, September 20, 2010.

Greenwalt, Bill, comments on "This Week in Defense News," January 4, 2009.

Halchin, L. Elaine, "Other Transaction (OT) Authority," Washington, D.C.: Congressional Research Service, January 27, 2010.

Haltiwanger, John C., Ron S. Jarmin, and Javier Miranda, "Who Creates Jobs? Small vs. Large vs. Young," National Bureau of Economic Research, Working Paper 16300, August 2010. As of February 16, 2012:
http://www.nber.org/papers/w16300

"HASC Defense Business Panel Holds San Diego Industry Roundtable," *Congressional Documents and Publications,* January 12, 2012.

Held, Bruce J., Thomas R. Edison, Jr., Shari Lawrence Pfleeger, Philip S. Antón, and John Clancy, *Evaluation and Recommendations for Improvement of the Department of Defense Small Business Innovation Research (SBIR) Program,* Santa Monica, Calif.: RAND Corporation, DB-490-OSD, 2006. As of July 21, 2011:
http://www.rand.org/pubs/documented_briefings/DB490

Horn, John, and Pleasance, Darren, "Restarting the US Small-business Growth Engine," *The McKinsey Quarterly,* November 2012. As of March 28, 2013:
https://www.mckinseyquarterly.com/Strategy/Growth/Restarting_the_US_small_business_growth_engine_3032

House Armed Services Committee (HASC) Panel on Business Challenges in the Defense Industry, "Challenges to Doing Business with the Department of Defense, Findings of the Panel of Business Challenges in the Defense Industry," March 19, 2012.

House Armed Services Committee, "Panel on Defense Acquisition Reform Findings and Recommendations," March 23, 2010. As of March 28, 2013:
http://faculty.nps.edu/danussba/docs/DefenseAcquisitionWorkforce_report_032310.pdf

"House Armed Services Committee Roundtable to Be Held at Rock Island Arsenal Schilling, Local Leaders to Participate," *Targeted News Service,* October 4, 2011.

"In Case You Missed It: House Armed Services Defense Business Panel Meets; Rep. Bobby Schilling (D-Il) News Release," *Congressional Documents and Publications,* October 7, 2011.

Jonas, Karen, "Local Businesses Speak with Members of Congress," *Santa Clarita Valley Signal*, January 9, 2012.

Lemnios, Zachary J., "Department of Defense Microelectronics Strategy," presentation atGOMACTech 2011, March 22, 2011.

Lichtblau, Eric, "New Earmark Rules Have Lobbyists Scrambling," *New York Times,* March 11, 2010.

Lorell, Mark A., *The U.S. Combat Aircraft Industry, 1909-2000: Structure, Competition, Innovation,* Santa Monica, Calif.: RAND Corporation, MR-1696-OSD, 2003. As of July 21, 2011:
http://www.rand.org/pubs/monograph_reports/MR1696.html

Lorell, Mark A., and Hugh P. Levaux, *The Cutting Edge: A Half Century of U.S. Fighter Aircraft R&D,* Santa Monica, Calif.: RAND Corporation, MR-939-AF, 1998. As of July 21, 2011:
http://www.rand.org/pubs/monograph_reports/MR939.html

Mandelbaum, Robb, "Will Obama 'QuickPay' Policy Mean Billions to Small Businesses?" *New York Times,* September 15, 2011. As of December 22, 2012:
http://boss.blogs.nytimes.com/2011/09/15/will-obama-quickpay-policy-mean-billions-to-small-businesses/

Matthews, William, "U.S House Aims to Reform Pentagon Service Contracts," *Defense News,* April 26, 2010. As of July 21, 2010:
http://www.defensenews.com/story.php?i=4593115&c=LAN&s=TOP

"Media Advisory: Congressmen Runyan and Shuster to Host Small Business Panel on Defense Contracting," *States News Service,* December 8, 2011.

Moore, Nancy Y., Clifford A. Grammich, Julie DaVanzo, Bruce J. Held, John Coombs, and Judith D. Mele, *Enhancing Small-Business Opportunities in the DoD,* Santa Monica, Calif.: RAND Corporation, TR-601-1-OSD, 2008. As of July 20, 2011:
http://www.rand.org/pubs/technical_reports/TR601-1.html

Naval Research Laboratory, *Fact Book 2010.* As of February 20, 2012:
http://www.nrl.navy.mil/content_images/factbook.pdf

"NJIT Procurement Director Makes DC Pitch for More Fed Funding," *States News Service,* December 13, 2011.

Office of Management and Budget, Office of Federal Procurement Policy, "Cost Accounting Standards Board Executive Compensation, Benchmark Maximum Allowable Amounts," 2013. As of January 23, 2013:
http://www.whitehouse.gov/omb/procurement_index_exec_comp

Office of the Deputy Under Secretary of Defense (Industrial Policy), *Transforming the Defense Industrial Base: A Roadmap,* February 2003. As of February 20, 2012:
http://www.dtic.mil/cgi-bin/GetTRDoc?AD=ADA492918

Office of the Under Secretary of Defense for Acquisition, Technology, and Logistics, "Creating an Effective National Security Industrial Base for the 21st Century: An Action Plan to Address the Coming Crisis," July 2008.

"Officials Outline Pentagon's Support to Industrial Base," *States News Service,* November 2, 2011.

Michael E. Porter, *Competitive Advantage: Creating and Sustaining Superior Performance,* New York: The Free Press, 1985.

Public Law 111-383, National Defense Authorization Act, 2011. As of July 20, 2011:
http://www.gpo.gov/fdsys/pkg/PLAW-111publ383/pdf/PLAW-111publ383.pdf

"Rep. West Brings Small Businesses Together with Defense Industry Experts," *States News Service,* February 21, 2012.

Rich, Michael D., *Evolution of the U.S. Defense Industry,* Santa Monica, Calif.: RAND Corporation P-7682, October 1990. As of July 21, 2011:
http://www.rand.org/pubs/papers/P7682.html

Roach, Emily, "Small Businesses Seek Slice of Pentagon Pie: U.S. House Members Try to Help Local Companies Get Chance at Defense Contracts," *Palm Beach Post,* February 22, 2012.

"Runyan Demands Fix for Small Businesses Contracting with DoD," *Targeted News Service,* February 21, 2012.

Rutherford, Emelie, "House to Weigh Bill Making Cost Bigger Factor in DoD Contract Contests," *Defense Daily,* April 28, 2010.

Serbu, Jared, "DoD to Create Map of Defense Industry," *Federal News Radio,* November 2, 2011.

Shuster, Representative Bill, "Small Business Critical to Defense Innovation," *The Hill,* January 24, 2012.

Templin, Carl R., and Michael E. Heberling, "Commercial Buying Practices in the Department of Defense: Barriers and Benefits," *International Journal of Purchasing and Materials Management,* Institute for Supply Management, February 1994. As of May 4, 2012:
http://www.ism.ws/pubs/JournalSCM/jscmarticle.cfm?ItemNumber=9764

Tiron, Roxanna, "Buy American Creates Hurdles for Pentagon's Business Plans," *The Hill,* November 26, 2006.

U.S. Air Force Chief Scientist, *Report on Technology Horizons: A Vision for Air Force Science & Technology During 2010–2030,* May 15, 2010. As of February 20, 2012:
http://www.af.mil/information/technologyhorizons.asp

U.S. Department of Commerce, U.S. Census Bureau, "Concordances," undated. As of March 28, 2013:
http://www.census.gov/eos/www/naics/concordances/concordances.html

U.S. Department of Commerce, U.S. Census Bureau, "Introduction to NAICS," 2012. As of March 28, 2013:
http://www.census.gov/eos/www/naics/

U.S. Department of Energy, "Technology Commercialization Fund." As of May 7, 2012:
http://techportal.eere.energy.gov/commercialization/technology_commercialization_fund.html

U.S. Department of State, Directorate of Defense Trade Controls, *International Traffic in Arms Regulations,* 2012. As of February 17, 2012:
http://pmddtc.state.gov/regulations_laws/itar_official.html

U.S. Code, Title 10, Section 2371, *Research Projects: Transactions Other than Contracts and Grants,* 2009. As of July 21, 2011:
http://www.gpo.gov/fdsys/pkg/USCODE-2009-title10/pdf/USCODE-2009-title10.pdf

U.S. House of Representatives, Panel on Defense Acquisition Reform, House Armed Services Committee, *Findings and Recommendations,* March 23, 2010.

"U.S. House Panel on Defense Industry to Hear from Hawaii Small Business," press release from Congresswoman Colleen Hanabusa, January 10, 2012.

U.S. House of Representatives, "Business Challenges within the Defense Industry: Hearing Before the Defense Financial Management and Auditability Reform Subcommittee," Washington, D.C., *Federal News Service Transcript,* September 20, 2011.

U.S. House of Representatives, "Creating a 21st Century Defense Industry: Hearing Before the House Armed Services Committee Panel on Business Challenges within the Defense Industry," Washington, D.C., *Federal News Service Transcript,* November 18, 2011.

U.S. House of Representatives, "Defense Industrial Base: Hearing Before the House Armed Services Committee Panel on Business Challenges within the Defense Industry," Washington, D.C., *CQ Transcriptions,* November 1, 2011.

U.S. House of Representatives, "The Defense Industrial Base: A National Security Imperative: Hearing Before the House Armed Services Committee Panel on Business Challenges within the Defense Industry," Washington, D.C., *Federal News Service Transcript,* October 24, 2011.

U.S. House of Representatives, "Opening Statement by Chairman Bill Shuster for Business Challenges within the Defense Industry: Hearing Before the Defense Financial Management and Auditability Reform Subcommittee," Washington, D.C., September 20, 2011.

U.S. House of Representatives, "Opening Statement by Chairman Bill Shuster for the Defense Industrial Base: A National Security Imperative: Hearing Before the House Armed Services Committee Panel on Business Challenges within the Defense Industry," Washington, D.C., October 24, 2011.

U.S. House of Representatives, "Opening Statement by Congressman Rick Larsen for Business Challenges within the Defense Industry: Hearing Before the Defense Financial Management and Auditability Reform Subcommittee," Washington, D.C., September 20, 2011.

U.S. House of Representatives, "Testimony Submitted by Andre J. Gudger for the Defense Industrial Base: Hearing Before the House Armed Services Committee Panel on Business Challenges within the Defense Industry," Washington, D.C., November 1, 2011.

U.S. House of Representatives, "Testimony Submitted by Barry Watts for the Defense Industrial Base: A National Security Imperative: Hearing Before the House Armed Services Committee Panel on Business Challenges within the Defense Industry," Washington, D.C., October 24, 2011.

U.S. House of Representatives, "Testimony Submitted by Bradford L. Smith for Business Challenges within the Defense Industry: Hearing Before the Defense Financial Management and Auditability Reform Subcommittee," Washington, D.C., September 20, 2011.

U.S. House of Representatives, "Testimony Submitted by Brett B. Lambert for the Defense Industrial Base: Hearing Before the House Armed Services Committee Panel on Business Challenges within the Defense Industry," Washington, D.C., November 1, 2011.

U.S. House of Representatives, "Testimony Submitted by David J. Berteau for Creating a 21st Century Defense Industry: Hearing Before the House Armed Services Committee Panel on Business Challenges within the Defense Industry," Washington, D.C., November 18, 2011.

U.S. House of Representatives, "Testimony Submitted by Frederick M. Downey for the Defense Industrial Base: A National Security Imperative: Hearing Before the House Armed Services Committee Panel on Business Challenges within the Defense Industry," Washington, D.C., October 24, 2011.

U.S. House of Representatives, Testimony of Ms. Heidi Jacobus, Chairman and CEO of Cybernet Systems Corporation on the merits of and deficiencies in the current SBIR program as applied to the Department of Defense hearing on "Challenges to Doing Business with the Department of Defense" before the Panel on Business Challenges Within the Defense Industry of the Committee on Armed Services, Washington, D.C., September 20, 2011. As of March 28, 2013:
http://armedservices.house.gov/index.cfm/files/serve?File_id=440222fe-430c-4c62-8529-7619d2badab3
see also:
http://www.gpo.gov/fdsys/pkg/CHRG-112hhrg70782/html/CHRG-112hhrg70782.htm

Wide Area Workflow, undated. As of March 29, 2013:
https://wawf.eb.mil/xhtml/unauth/web/homepage/FunctionalInfo.xhtml